CW00918765

Everyday Life and the Unconscious Mind

Everyday Life and the Unconscious Mind

An Introduction to Psychoanalytic Concepts

Hannah Curtis

Routledge
Taylor & Francis Group
LONDON AND NEW YORK

First published 2015 by
Karnac Books Ltd.

Published 2018 by Routledge
2 Park Square, Milton Park, Abingdon, Oxon OX14 4RN
711 Third Avenue, New York, NY 10017, USA

Routledge is an imprint of the Taylor & Francis Group, an informa business

British Library Cataloguing in Publication Data

A C.I.P. for this book is available from the British Library

ISBN-13: 9781782201946 (pbk)

Typeset by V Publishing Solutions Pvt Ltd., Chennai, India

CONTENTS

CONTENTS

INTRODUCTION

It was a Friday afternoon, the end of the week and I had been leading a seminar with a group of mature students who were undertaking a degree course in therapeutic communication. We had been discussing the use of psychotherapeutic approaches in their work with challenging and vulnerable young people. The seminar came to an end and I began to think of going home, unwinding for the weekend and turning my attention to personal and family events. At last it was time to switch off and relax. As I pulled on my coat one of the students said, "Hannah, what is transference? I just can't get my head around this transference business, I don't get it." Her challenge was joined by a chorus of voices saying "I don't get it either, every time I use it in an essay I get a margin comment that says *this is not transference,* so what is it?"

Another voice piped up, "And I don't understand the difference between countertransference and projective identification, can you explain that as well?"

They wanted a succinct and accurate definition that they could understand and use, in essays and in their daily work with children and young adults in emotional distress.

My fondly imagined escape to the weekend was put on hold as I attempted to offer the briefest of explanations of these concepts in the shortest time possible.

The students generously acknowledged that they understood better when we finished, but I went home feeling somewhat dissatisfied that I had not done justice to such important and useful concepts, and that I needed to find a way of addressing their complexity with simplicity and everyday thinking. I began by writing three short papers that became the last three chapters of this book. I did not realise that a book was in the making, I was just sorting out my thoughts.

But, as is the way with psychoanalytic thinking, one thing led to another. It was not long before the notion that it might be useful to write more, began to take hold. To some extent this notion was based on my own experience of being a social worker, and subsequently wishing that I had had an understanding of these concepts to support me when I was doing such difficult and emotionally draining work. Psychoanalytic thinking would have helped me to make sense of the demands of the professional task, not only directly in contact with clients and colleagues, but also in managing my own feelings. In other words, I would have been strengthened by such a framework for thinking, and that would have made me more confident, more solid and less anxious. A little less anxiety would, I believe, have released more energy to work more creatively.

Hence the book became an introduction to the concepts that I wish I had been able to draw upon, and that I do now draw upon, in my daily working life. It includes those that are applicable to everyday encounters with colleagues and with those who call upon our services in our working environment, whatever that may be. It is to do with the ways in which we all bring our own psychological selves to every aspect of our relational interactions with others. It is to do with having a framework within which to think about what others may be bringing to their interactions with us. I believe that such a framework supports people in being able to think carefully,

in becoming more able to see the
are engaged in complicated and puzz

All of the concepts that are introc
book have been formed, developed, e
the context of the work that takes place
or psychotherapist and the person with
There are many books available that fulfil
the reader to the application of psychoanaly
thinking to a therapy relationship, but this b   the application of psychoanalysis to everyday life as opposed to its use in
the consulting room. Such concepts are applicable to other forms
of relational work, and indeed to ordinary every day encounters.
In my experience they help to make for a richer and more honest
connection with others, at all levels of relationship.

I hope that a book like this might be useful to a range of people who undertake the difficult and demanding work of becoming
involved with those in our society who are vulnerable, and challenging. There are increasing numbers of people who struggle with
emotional and psychological distress, from very small children to
the elderly. We know that mental health problems affect everyone
across the social spectrum. We desperately need to be able to think
about their state of mind and how it interacts with our own if we
are to offer them a human connection that is supportive and helpful. We need to be able to make some sense of what lies beyond the
apparent behaviour, not just in them but also in ourselves.

The book began as a book for people with no clinical training,
who work with the most vulnerable members of our society. It is
not a scholarly book and I am aware that in some respects it does
not do full justice to the complexities of each concept, to the difference of opinions about each concept, or to the degree to which
psychoanalysis has developed and continues to develop. Psychoanalysis today is a rigorous and highly disciplined school of thought

…academic standards, but it is my hope that this book
…ul to those who work at the coal face, to employers in
…e sector, to the general public who are interested in how
…eir colleagues or employees may be thinking and feeling about
the work that they do, and to students of psychoanalysis who simply find the subject as fascinating as I do.

It is for, and because of, my students, particularly those students who ask the apparently simple but actually most challenging questions.

ACKNOWLEDGEMENTS

Nobody writes a book without a lot of support, encouragement and help from others. I have my students to thank for the inspiration. My very dear friend Glynis Gadd, read all the chapters, commenting, correcting, and challenging each one as it developed. Some of her comments were integrated into the final version and some were not.

I also have to thank Laura Pearse and Timothy Phillips for reading, commenting, and offering feedback on the final draft.

As always I have to thank my husband Alan, who unfailingly sees me through everything.

ONE

The background to the conscious and unconscious aspects of the mind

Sigmund Freud's working life spanned well over fifty years. Between 1886 and 1939 when he died, he produced twenty-four volumes of work that formed the foundation stones of the discipline to which he gave the name "psychoanalysis". His adult life was characterised by a huge output of work and the development of many ideas and ways of thinking. He was one of the most original and brilliant thinkers of all time. He effected a revolution in the way in which we think about, and understand ourselves and our relationships with others. Other brilliantly clever historical figures, such as Newton, Galileo, Einstein, Darwin, have revolutionised the way in which we understand the world around us, but Freud is the person who radically changed forever, the way in which we understand and can think about, the world within ourselves. This revolution has had a profound impact upon our personal, social, and political lives. Psychoanalysis has something to say about the everyday detail of the most ordinary humdrum life and something to say about the momentous events of war and of social change. It has something to say about the intimacy of the new born infant's relationship to the mother, and about how this can link to an ambition to be powerful, to rule a nation, to subject others to one's own will.

It is a difficult subject to attempt to study because not only is there a lot to study, but it is complex and it has evolved and is evolving all the time. There are never any absolutes in psychoanalysis, and it continues to be a discipline in which, and about which there is debate, argument, and disagreement. There are old ideas being regenerated and new ideas being put forward, and this keeps the study of psychoanalysis fresh and pertinent to modern day life. All the schools of psychological thought that thrive today began with psychoanalysis. It was the precursor of cognitive psychology, behavioural psychology, neurological psychology, forensic psychology. All the different types of therapy and therapeutic interventions that have started up, faded or thrived, began with psychoanalysis and it is not possible to begin to think about how people function psychologically and emotionally without acknowledging Freud and his ongoing influence in this field.

Psychoanalysis is both a discipline for understanding the way in which we function in the world and a method of treatment, but it is from the treatment that the understanding grows. It is from listening to patients in the consulting room, and attending carefully to what they are conveying, that the ideas, the theories, and body of knowledge has built up. It is from the attempt to help people with their internal conflicts, that we have learned over many years something about how the mental life of the individual, and the group, operates.

It was originally developed on three fronts. It was a procedure by which unconscious mental processes could be investigated. The methodological model for this was simple, the analyst invited the patient to say whatever was on their mind without attempting to edit out any thoughts or images that came to mind. It was also a method of treatment for "neurotic" symptoms, the treatment being the understanding of the symbolic meaning of the symptoms as a result of the careful attention to the patients "free associations" as they were called. This is no quick treatment, but if it is continued for long enough and changes can be observed and experienced, it can profoundly alter and enrich the emotional and psychological life of the individual and of those amongst whom they live. These two strands can then be used as the basis for an authentic and experiential method of collecting and examining information about human functioning on a broader scale, which is the third front.

There is not room to go any further into these aspects of psychoanalysis here as to do so would take the discussion away from its purpose which is to think about the idea of an unconscious mind, but there is one feature of trying to understand psychoanalysis which does matter here at the beginning. This is that there is an inherent frustration and requirement for patience in trying to learn about psychoanalysis, because there are many strands. These strands need to be separated out and thought through and understood independently of the other strands in order to be clear about them and to distinguish them one from another. But the problem with this is that they are also interlinked with each other, and it is not really possible to fully grasp the meaning of one concept without doing so in relation to another, and another and so on.

The student, (and indeed the learned person, for this is not a subject that lends itself to ever being fully comprehended) has to be prepared to tolerate a sense of not understanding something very well until one has got to its related concepts and has started to be able to bring them together and to see how they may fit into the bigger picture.

Even then there is the fact that the concepts as they were originally conceived have undergone development and modification, and these developments have not been the same in all countries, or in all the psychological disciplines, so that it is the case that a concept can be defined in one way by one person and another way by another person, and neither is absolutely right or wrong. This is a strength and a weakness of psychoanalysis. There is strength in its capacity to be used, rethought, and reworked, and a weakness in its difficulty in ever being finally defined or proven.

These features make it undeniably interesting, thought provoking, and intellectually challenging. It is nothing if not a dynamic and a provocative discipline, and it has the capacity to offer profound insights into the nature of the human person and human relationships.

Perhaps one of the most remarkable achievements of Freud's work, and from this examination of the mind, was to make us all realise that we have a large part of our mind that is unconscious. We now take for granted the fact that we all have aspects of our thinking and our feelings, of which we are entirely unaware. We take this so much for granted that it is as though this was always known, there was never a time when people did not realise this. Indeed many thinkers before Freud did acknowledge an unconscious aspect of the mind and it has always been the stuff of poetry, philosophy, literature, and the arts, but it was Freud who thought about it and wrote about in a way that made such an idea available to the general populace, and enabled us all to take ownership of such a way of understanding ourselves and others.

Freud (1915e) developed a model of the mind that divided it into three areas of consciousness; the conscious, the subconscious, and the unconscious. This is known as the topographical model. The conscious part of our mind is that of awareness. We know what we are consciously thinking and feeling. We know what is on our mind at any given moment. If we are choosing something to have for our lunch we know that we are thinking about food and what we might enjoy or what we think would be good for us.

We may also have some awareness of what it is that influences those decisions. We may realise that we are choosing a particular dish for lunch because we have tried it before and enjoyed it. In the back of our minds we may have a memory of eating that dish, of the circumstances in which we ate it and the associations that we have to that dish. We may realise that one of the reasons that we are choosing that particular dish for lunch is that it is associated with some good memories. Freud would have considered that this awareness comes from the subconscious part of our mind, a part of the mind to which we have easy access but is not at the forefront of our thinking.

But there may be even more to our decision about which dish to eat. There may be influences which are completely unconscious and buried deeply in our psyche. For example there may be some totally forgotten memory of moments of intimacy involving food. We may have had the pleasure of having shared times of profoundly loving intimacy whilst being fed by our mother as an infant, and this intimacy may be what we unconsciously look for in making a choice about which dish to eat, we may actually be trying to decide which food is most likely to offer us that sense of intimate loving pleasure that exists in our experience but we have since forgotten. This experience is retained but not easily remembered. It is known, but it is not readily accessible to conscious thought. It is unconscious.

This idea of the mind can be likened to an iceberg. Most of an iceberg is below the surface of the water and unseen to the eye. Only a small aspect of it is visible above the surface. Freud considered that the mind operated mostly at an unconscious level and that only a small part of it is conscious or available to consciousness.

Because of the work that Freud and his successors have done over the years, we now take for granted the fact that our behaviour is sometimes ordered by our experiences in early life. We also understand that one event in our day can have an impact upon how we handle another event and that we may not be aware of this process. If we are in a good mood, we carry that mood with us to the different encounters that we have with other people. We do not necessarily think about it but we know it is there. We know that we have an unconscious life, but we are not aware of it all the time.

That we realise that we do have this unconscious life, is due to the impact that Sigmund Freud and the discipline of psychoanalysis, has had on our understanding of how people's emotional lives operate. This awareness is so embedded in our assumptions about ourselves and each other that on the whole we do not give it very much conscious attention and it is easy to be unaware of the fact that it needed somebody to realise this and to give it a name, for us to be able to conceptualise such a feature of everyday life.

Poets, philosophers, story tellers, all made good use of the phenomenon of unconscious processes in their thinking and writing. Fairy tales speak to the unconscious fears and fantasies of children. Murder mysteries, books and films about frightening events, and nail biting tension, tap into the unconscious fears and fantasies of adults. We are attracted to these fictional tales because they link powerfully with something inside all of us, of which we remain consciously unaware, but which responds to these aspects of our cultural life and to which we are drawn by an invisible and somewhat irresistible cord.

In thinking about this unconscious aspect of the mind Freud went on through his life to think about and write about aspects of human functioning which we encounter in everyday life. He wrote about love and hate, dreams, jokes, slips of the tongue, all those small everyday events that we tend to ignore and consider unremarkable. Freud put these events on the agenda for psychological discussion. He turned them from unimportant and easily dismissed features of people's lives into subjects for research, evidence of an unconscious life, and expressions of the depths of the mind of which we are normally unaware.

Love and hate are not small matters, they are the feelings that organise the way in which we live. The friends that we choose are those for whom we have loving feelings, the partner with whom we decide to live and to have children is someone towards whom we feel love and that decision profoundly affects the rest of our lives.

On the other hand if what we feel is mostly hate, we are likely to be destructive in our connection to the world around us. We may get into fights with people, we may steal or break or hurt. Decisions about how to behave are based primarily on whether we approach the world in which we live from the basis of loving feelings, or care, or whether we approach it from the basis of hateful feelings, or not caring.

Freud (1900a) wrote two volumes on dreams, a huge amount of work. He described dreams as being "the royal road to the unconscious". He considered that dreams and dreaming were the products of the unconscious mind that emerged in sleep when the conscious mind is at rest. He thought that they were the way in which our emotional experiences can be processed, and in which unresolved conflicts can be expressed, albeit in symbolic imagery. He thought that dreams are a lot more than this and that this is yet another area of thinking about the life of the unconscious mind.

If we think about why we laugh when someone makes a joke, it is usually because the punch line takes us by surprise. It takes us by surprise in a way that we find pleasurable. Not everyone finds the same joke to be funny and this is because they connect with it differently, but this is rarely a conscious thing.

Unless we have decided beforehand that we are not going to enjoy someone's joke, we will be taken by surprise and will find that either enjoyable and laugh, or we may find it unenjoyable and feel mildly or strongly disgusted by it. A joke works because it says something unexpected, and this triggers an involuntary response, which we enjoy.

We also often find slips of the tongue to be funny. This is because they often reveal what we really think rather than what we consciously intended to say.

Such errors of speech are now so associated with Freud as to be commonly termed "Freudian slips". This is especially the case when the error is such that the word that is actually used has some sexual connotation. An example would be when someone like a politician says "we must give our children the breast education" rather than the "best education".

Since Freud put these features of everyday life on the map, they have been debated, disagreed with, and discussed endlessly, and this continues to be the case. I do not intend here to enter into these debates, my point here is to acknowledge that he did put them on the map and that they remain there and that we now appreciate that such expressions of an unconscious aspect of the mind are not nothing, they are something and they do have significance. They are aspects of human functioning that are worthy of research, study and careful thought.

Freud (1923b) also developed another very simple, but useful, model of the mind that he termed the structural model. This model sits within the topographical model and consists of three aspects.

The first is what he called the id.

The id is present from birth and is to do with basic instinctual human drives, the most basic of which is the survival instinct. When the infant cries she is demanding to be fed immediately. She has no capacity to wait patiently.

In later life the sexual drive can be experienced in a very similar way, there is an urgency, a demand for immediate satisfaction of the desire, the drive to achieve sexual release. This can be thought of as an instinctual drive since it is such a fundamental aspect of human functioning and relationships. The id impulses quickly come to be linked psychologically with the seeking of a pleasurable state of being. When the infant is fed, burped, and comfortable, she is happy. She can sleep contentedly, or gurgle, or look around and engage with her surroundings. As she grows she will increasingly do these things, so long as she is happy, so long as her id impulses are satisfied. Even as a small baby of maybe just weeks or months old, if her experience has been of not being able to feel fed, warm and comfortable, she will need to keep seeking the satisfaction of these basic instinctual needs and may be delayed in her capacity to begin to develop from this stage.

Again we can see a connection with the sexual drive here. When a person is in need of sexual satisfaction they cannot readily think of anything else until that drive, that desire, that pleasure, is satisfied.

Whilst the id is in the first instance to do with the basic instinctual drive to survive, it is also to do with the drive to have ones wishes, desires and impulses gratified without impediment. Whilst this is necessary for the small infant, it is evident that this situation cannot continue, the infant will in time have to discover that life cannot be one continuous experience of having everything one's own way. Most parents will intuitively begin to introduce their infants to the experience of having to wait, having to tolerate a degree of frustration. This is the beginning of learning that we have to cooperate with the other people in our environment in order for everyone to have their needs and wishes met to a reasonable degree.

In response to the need to learn to control and modify our early primitive wishes and desires, we need an aspect of our mind that can influence and curb the id. This is called the ego.

The ego is that part of the personality that recognises reality and on the basis of this recognition decides if the instinctual wish can be gratified or not. If the wish is unacceptable it will be blocked by the ego. For example angry feelings can often be accompanied by a wish to be violent, to seriously hurt the person who is perceived as being to blame for the anger. We may even feel like murdering that person. If we have a reasonably well functioning ego, we will not take this step. There will be an aspect of personality that argues that this would not be a good step to take, and that eventually prevails over the id. The ego is the voice of reason, the sensible mediating aspect that can recognise an unacceptable wish emanating from the id and move into place some thinking about the reasons for that wish to not be gratified. It will do this with the assistance of defence mechanisms, in response to an awareness of a sense of anxiety, a feeling that gratification of the wish may bring unwanted trouble with it. It is this reasoning that helps to make acceptable the non-gratification of a wish, helps to make it bearable.

The ego is the part of our mind that we use in a conscious way, to help us to make decisions and choices. When we are thinking about the best choice to make we are using our ego. It also has an important role in negotiating between the id and the superego, which is the third aspect of the mind in the structural model.

The superego is essentially to do with the development of a conscience. It is that aspect of our personality that does learn to care about others, to feel guilty when we cause harm, to choose to forego our own desires rather than inflict hurt on someone else.

The id and the superego are mediated by the ego, which functions as a sort of arbitrator between the id and the superego. When there is a conflict between the wish that is seeking gratification, and the guilt that is attached to that wish, the ego can attempt to negotiate a compromise, a solution to the dilemma that is acceptable to both parties. The person who is so enraged that they feel like murdering someone, may settle for smashing a few plates instead. In this way their id based frustration can find expression, whilst their superego/conscience can remain clear.

But the superego can become something of a tyrannical ruler for some people, just as the id can for others. Some people are so dominated by an internal rule book full of shoulds and shouldn'ts that they are unable to contemplate the possibility of taking any risks in their lives.

I know of someone like this. She is so anxious about doing the wrong thing that she barely does anything. She is very quiet, rarely contributes to a conversation, has never pursued new employment opportunities even though she is intelligent, and has never considered having any lover other than her husband. We could say that she is lacking in self-confidence, which indeed she is, but what she experiences is a sense of being controlled by the need to be good, and the ever present danger of behaving badly, improperly or in a way that others would find distasteful. She is constantly guarding against a superego that is harsh in its moral condemnation of any wishes or desires that she may have that do not accord with what another person might want of her.

This person has a harsh superego and her ego is not up to the job of negotiating with that. Her superego always wins.

For most reasonably emotionally mature adults there is a balance between the id, the ego, and the superego. A kind of negotiation goes on with the ego as a mediator and a voice of reason.

We could return here to the everyday question of how we choose what to eat at a mealtime. We have touched upon the notion that the choices that we make about the food we eat may well involve the conscious, sub or pre conscious, and the unconscious mind. In other words that the whole of our mind is involved in this daily decision but that we are only aware of a small area of that process of decision making. If we now think about such an ordinary decision keeping in mind the structural model we can begin to examine the way in which the id, the ego, and superego, and the relationship between these three aspects of the mind as described in the structural model, influence such a decision.

We can also consider that this is not just a very personal issue, but that the matter of what we eat is actually a huge cultural issue and an important factor in the health of a nation and the demands on social resources such as health services. This makes it an important area of everyday life to study.

We have an obesity epidemic taking place throughout the western world.

This indicates that many people find it very difficult to restrict their food intake, they eat too much. This could be thought about as an id dominated epidemic, in which a lot of people cannot say no to their desire to keep on eating beyond what they need and what is healthy for them. Because food is plentiful and delicious, we have to make many decisions every day about what to eat and how much to eat. This is a feature of our everyday lives. So every day, several times per day we may have to negotiate between the wish to continue enjoying more food than we really need and the knowledge that to do so is not good for our health. The fact that we have an obesity crisis suggests that a lot of people find this negotiation very tricky to manage and give in to their id. But we may also hear those same people saying things like, "I really shouldn't eat this but –"Then we can hear the debate between the id and the superego taking place and the id wins. What is not happening is an effective contribution by the ego in which a more rational choice is made based on what is healthy in the long run.

Eating patterns and people's relationships with food are very complicated and this equation that I have put forward here is one part of a bigger picture to illustrate the point rather than to explain the difficulties that people have with eating.

But to continue with this example, perhaps what then happens on a large social scale is that many people develop health problems as a result of their eating and weight. Then they need to be cared for, nursed, and treated as someone who is unwell. In Britain we are often hearing about how stretched the NHS services are, how demand is very much greater than supply. It would seem that the nursing, medical care that people require is much greater than the available resources. If we return here to the previous part of the chapter in which we thought about how the choice of lunch might actually be linked to a deeper unconscious search for an experience of loving intimacy, then we could begin to wonder if the phenomenon of eating habits that lead to medical problems which in turn lead to medical care, might also be to do with a general need within our current population to find a source of care, nurturing, some kind of experience of having someone who is concerned about us, worried about us, attending to us. Maybe this is what we seek when we overeat, an emotional experience of being lovingly attended to. Maybe this is why we call it comfort eating. If this is the case then the next question has to be about a great many people feeling that they do not get enough loving care in their life. We can question why this may be and we can wonder about the effects of this sense of not being well enough loved. One result would seem to be that they are then less able to develop a strong enough ego to negotiate their own internal conflicts and to think through their everyday emotional dilemmas in such a way as to make decisions that work in the interests of their health and well-being.

One question leads to another and another, and the next question might be about whether someone who cannot make good decisions for themselves is then able to make good decisions on behalf of others. For example if someone cannot make good food choices for themselves, will they be able to do so for their children? Does the cycle of poor ego functioning get repeated and visited upon the next generation?

We are told that an increasing number of children are now obese, so it would seem that this cycle is indeed in place, that at least in the area of food and eating, the capacity to regulate intake and make healthy choices is a diminishing skill. It could be argued that we are a more id dominated society in this respect at least.

The question of food and eating and its meaning to each of us as individuals, is much more complex than this, but it is an everyday event with which we all engage and we can think about it in these terms whilst simultaneously appreciating that this is by no means the whole story. It is an example of how the unconscious and conscious structure of our mind is engaged in a daily way and in daily choices.

I hope that in this chapter I have introduced the reader to something of the background to psychoanalytic thinking and to two conceptual areas that act as a frame for the development of psychoanalysis from its beginnings. These concepts of conscious, subconscious, and unconscious aspects of the mind, the topographic model, help us to have a sense of the depth of the mind and of having degrees of access to it.

The structural model offers a way of thinking about how our mind has developed through infancy to adulthood, again three layers of maturity that interact with each other. We are not conscious of this interaction necessarily, but we use it all the time. The decisions, dilemmas, and conflicts that we experience every day, in small ways and large are navigated through these aspects of our mind, and how well they function has a huge bearing upon our capacity to think and to make intelligent choices.

Since Freud's death in 1939, the field of psychoanalysis has grown and become increasingly sophisticated. These models that were developed then, remain valid and useful tools to have in mind as we negotiate our relationships and interaction with others in our daily lives.

TWO

Trauma

It could be argued that all forms of emotional distress, from mild upset to major mental health problems, are caused by, or triggered by some form of trauma. The word trauma comes from the Greek word "wound". Originally it would have referred to a physical wound but is just as often now thought of as a psychological wound. A physical wound is an injury that breaks the protective barrier of the skin and causes damage to that which lies beneath the surface. This can be mild damage that can heal easily, or it can be severe damage that will need time and treatment for recovery to take place.

In this chapter I will consider what it is that constitutes an emotional trauma, that it can be an unusual and extreme event, and it can be an everyday almost unnoticeable event that can trigger traumatised responses. The damage of a trauma can be fairly minor or it can have long term emotional consequences and I hope to look at the ways in which the impact of a traumatic event works in the mind of an individual and can then be present in everyday interactions with the people in one's environment.

It is relatively straightforward to recognise extreme instances of trauma and to imagine how awful they must be. If someone is involved in a serious car accident the trauma to their body may be great. The body may be broken literally and it will take time, skill, and care to repair the effects of the traumatic event. We can also recognise that the person will need time and care to recover from the emotional effects of such a trauma. It is not difficult to empathise with such an event and to imagine how we might feel if it were to happen to us.

But there are many painful events that are not so obviously noticeable. There are many shocks to the system, hurts and humiliations that everyone suffers in different ways. One of the factors that really matters, is not the hurts, the wounds, the shocks themselves, but our own individual capacities to cope with them. Some people are devastated by events that are painful and out of their control and others are more able to withstand such events. Our individual capacity to cope with trauma will be influenced not only by our own innate personal strength, but also by the relationships that we have through our lives with those who are in a position to either promote and develop that strength, or to attack and undermine it.

If we have known the experience of being supported and helped through a trauma we can grow and learn from it, but if our emotional responses to trauma have been misunderstood or dismissed or even punished, we will not have been given the opportunity to remember and work through and we will be much more likely to repeat, to act out, to express our feelings in confusing and sometimes unacceptable ways.

It is trauma, in all sorts of forms and how we deal with them, that is at the heart of the development of defence mechanisms. It is trauma, large and small, that needs to be remembered in order to be worked through rather than repeated. It is central to an understanding of how we function psychologically because in using the term "deal with it" I do not mean dealing with it in any practical or conscious or observable sense, but how we deal with it internally, in the depths of our unconscious psyche.

A psychoanalytic understanding of the meaning of trauma has been developed from the casework that has been undertaken with patients in therapy who have undergone extreme trauma, such as being trapped in a burning building, being on board a sinking ship. These are useful experiences to study because they are very specific identifiable instances of an unusual and clearly traumatic event. A psychoanalytic understanding of the meaning and importance of traumatic events has been developed by listening to people who survive such events and by trying to notice how they process them, both in the short term and in the long term. As result we can begin to apply this understanding to the smaller everyday traumas that occur frequently.

When I was a young mother myself, I remember a very ordinary sort of school day morning. I had delivered my children to school and as I was leaving I noticed a mother coming towards me with a pushchair and three or four small children around her. I did not know her well but I did know that she was a child-minder and that the older children that she had with her were minded children that she was taking to school. She was a little late and seemed very harassed. I noticed that one of the small children was a new child that I had not seen before. He was about three years old. She stopped ahead of me and said to the new child, in a very strict tone, "You *will* hold onto the pushchair". She then turned her attention to the other children, so that she did not see the expression of fear that crossed the child's face as it crumpled into despair. She did not see the shudder that passed through his little body, or the way in which he looked around as if to try to find something. I continued to watch the little boy as they walked towards me and he seemed bewildered, and frightened as he clung very tightly to the pushchair. They passed by me and I did not watch them any further.

The child-minder had not been particularly unkind, she was concerned for his safety on a busy street with a lot of parents and children milling around. She was not being violent or even very aggressive, perhaps harsh and unsympathetic, but not cruel. But it occurred to me at that time that I had been an observer to a traumatic event in that little boy's life, or perhaps more accurately, a traumatic moment. It is likely that if that was his first day with a new child-minder he may have continued to feel bewildered, a bit lost and to be wondering when his mummy would return.

I also wondered how he would process that traumatic moment. He was too young to be able to describe it to his mother or father later in the day, and the child-minder had not noticed it happening. Nobody was aware of the fact that he had been frightened and so nobody was able to offer him comfort and reassurance. This sort of mini trauma must happen to small children all the time and at an age when they do not have the verbal mechanisms with which to convey their worries to an adult except by crying, and this might not be met with understanding or sympathy but with impatience or even rejection or further punishment.

I wondered how such a small child would process that sort of event emotionally. It may be that his relationship with his parents or carers was very strong and that he was able to have a sense of certainty that his mother and father would not have left him with someone who would not treat him well. If so he might have been able to draw upon this certainty to support him through his first bewildering day. John Bowlby (1958) developed a way of identifying levels of emotional security in his work on Attachment Theory. But if the little boy did not have an internal feeling of emotional security, it may be that this small event would be taken in by him emotionally and sort of stored as an aspect of himself. He would then have an experience of himself as a frightened confused little boy who needed to behave very well to avoid anything more frightening happening. If he then has further small traumatic events that layer upon this one, this sense of being a frightened confused person could build into a more substantial aspect of personality and gradually become a part of the person's identity.

In respect of this particular little boy I have no idea what the event with the pushchair might have meant to him, as I did not know him at all. My hypothesis is based on knowing something about psychoanalytic theory and this makes a lot of sense to me, but I was struck by the observation and the thought that many small traumas take place in a child's life that nobody ever notices.

At the other end of the spectrum, there are more easily identifiable traumatic events. When two aeroplanes were hijacked and deliberately flown into the World Trade Centre buildings in New York in September 2001, almost six thousand people were killed and injured. Those who survived were terrified for their lives. Kevin Kelly (2012) has written about his work as a therapist with some of the firefighters who worked to save lives when this attack occurred. His account records the long term emotional conflicts that this experience triggered for those men and their families as they struggled to make sense of the way in which their world had been invaded and so comprehensively trashed. This event traumatised many people and shocked the whole world. As the decades roll on, the traumatic effects of that event still reverberate, still echo around the community, the country and the rest of the world.

It was a world changing event, things could never be the same again. This is a feature of a trauma, it feels as though it changes everything. Not only is the world a different place but the self is different. We are altered by trauma, and the person that we were before the trauma is not the person we become in the aftermath of trauma. This is not always apparent until sometime after the trauma has passed.

I want to look at how and why trauma can be life changing and what it is that the little boy that I observed in the street, has in common with someone directly affected by an event as huge as the collapse of the World Trade Centre. In this way I hope to show how trauma is a universal and everyday experience and how it contributes to our everyday interactions.

When the little boy discussed above, let us call him Billy, woke up on the morning of the day that I noticed him, it is very likely that he awoke in his own bed, that he felt safe, warm, and that he was confident that his Mummy and Daddy were there and that his breakfast would be available for him. Of course it may not have been like this but I intend to suppose this for the sake of demonstrating the process by which a trauma is felt. It is very likely that he felt secure in the knowledge that his daily life and his own little world would be as he expected it to be. He may have been told about going to a new child minder, he may have met her and spent time with her and other children, but at such a young age he may not have had a concept of being with a new person for a whole day, or of what a lot of new knowledge he would have to take in, in order to get used to his new circumstances of spending more time with this child minder. There may well have been a number of new circumstances to adapt to. A different house, several other children arriving before school, having to get coats and shoes on with a number of other children milling around, and not least, no one familiar in the immediate vicinity. Billy's sense of not knowing the place, the people, the routine, and what was expected of him would have been developing for a while. By the time I saw him he had probably already had an hour or so of feeling that he did not fully understand what was going on around him, and did not know how or where he fitted in to the bigger picture. The brief interaction that I witnessed was not overtly cruel but it was not kindly either and what I thought I saw in Billy's reaction was an experience of feeling that a tipping point had been reached, that he had reached the limit of his capacity to feel and tolerate his feelings of confusion. Up until then he had been bewildered and confused, but not scared. When he was spoken to harshly he experienced a sense of fear. The question for us in this hypothetical reconstruction, is to do with the nature of that fear, what was Billy afraid of?

Before addressing this question I want to think a little about the New York firefighter on the morning of September 11th 2001, and in particular about his wife, in a similarly hypothetical way, but also to follow the progression of psychological events that build into a trauma. I hope to explain how the psychological, emotional, processes involved in an everyday minor trauma such as Billy's can be very much the same as those in a huge dramatic trauma. They can be the same but on a different scale, and this is the case for an adult and for a child.

Jack, the firefighter, starts his day in a fairly usual way. He gets up, dresses, breakfasts, sees his children off to school, and prepares to go to work. He and his family know that in his job every day is different. Some days nothing much happens and on other days there is a serious situation in which he has to take great care to ensure that he and his colleagues are safe whilst they attempt to secure the safety of others and to put out fires. He and the family have become accustomed to this level of risk in his job and it does not actively worry them on a daily basis. Jack also protects his family sometimes from a full awareness of what his work can entail. They all assume that later in the day they will be together again for supper when the events of the day will be recounted to each other.

Jack's wife, Monica, leaves for her job as a legal secretary in a law firm. Later in the morning a friend calls her and says,

"Have you heard?" Monica becomes alert to the possibility that something is wrong, she is alert but nothing more at this point. Her friend then tells her that there has been some terrible attack on the World Trade Centre and the whole of lower Manhattan is being evacuated. Monica knows at this point that her husband Jack may have been called to this situation, but she does not know how serious it is. She is confused, worried but not frightened. She tells her colleague. Her colleague suggests that they see if the TV is broadcasting anything about it. It is. As Monica watches the screen the full horror of the attacks on these buildings begins to seep into her awareness. She gradually has the thought that this is a very big and very devastating event. She also realises that every firefighter in New York will have been called to it and that it will probably overwhelm their capacity to contain the damage and to save lives. She probably realises that her husband's life is in more danger than either of them had ever imagined possible.

There are stages in this process of realisation. In the first stage as the family leave for their daily work, they carry with them a sense of assurance. They are confident that they will see each other at supper. We all need this level of assurance, in order to go out we need to be reasonably sure that we will return home. When Monica gets the call from a friend her sense of assurance is not particularly undermined. Her friend might be about to tell her some gossip that does not really matter to her, but she is alert to the possibility that it is more serious than that. Then her sense of assurance, of confidence that her day will end much as it began, gradually starts to unravel. As it does so, Monica takes emotional steps backwards and forwards. She learns that something awful has happened and she thinks of Jack, but she quickly tells herself that he is highly trained and experienced and knows what he is doing. Anyway he might not be there. Then her sense of assurance is attacked again as she learns a little more about what has happened. She has to find room in her mind for the awareness that Jack will most certainly be there, but again he always puts safety first and would not risk his own life. But actually he might risk his own life, rather than leave someone in danger. But no, don't think about that, wait and see, Jack always comes home and today will be no different. But today is different, everyone is shouting, running, another plane has flown into the 2nd building, the world as Monica knows it, has collapsed. The unthinkable, the unimaginable, the impossible, has happened. Monica begins to tremble, she stares at the TV screen with her hand over her open mouth. She cannot move, she cannot think, her whole being is overwhelmed by the enormity of what she is seeing and the knowledge that the man she loves is almost certainly in the thick of it. What Monica is doing in this psychological process is struggling with the internal conflict of trying to allow her mind to accept the reality that she is facing, but at the same time trying to deny that reality in order to maintain a sense that the world is as she knows it to be. She is really struggling with a feeling of madness, because suddenly nothing is as it should be. What she has always known is no longer reality, and yet what has become reality makes no sense to her.

After a few minutes she suddenly comes to and thinks of her children. Do they know what is happening? Are they ok? She decides to go home. In her confusion, bewilderment and fear, she feels a desperate need to be in her own home, where she can feel safe, where things are as they have always been, and where her family will need her to be. She wants to be in a place that makes sense, and this she equates with her home.

Little Billy probably wanted to go home too. He too may have felt his world unravel as little by little he found that he did not understand where he was, why he was doing what he was doing, and then in the moments that I watched him, a sense of psychological collapse and fear. He too may have found his own three-year-old way of reassuring himself as much as he could up to a point, but eventually been overwhelmed by the changes in his day, and the amount of unfamiliarity that he had to accommodate. When a child is frightened, or hurt, or confused, they too look for the environment in which they feel safe and which makes sense to them. For children this is usually their mummy or daddy.

The feeling state that Monica was seeking, was the same as the feeling state that Billy wanted. It was one of safety, and it was sought in response to a feeling of overwhelming emotional collapse. In Monica's case the world really was being turned upside down. In Billy's case he was just too little to understand it all. But the emotional turmoil, though on different scales, was of the same order.

There are many examples of trauma that fall between these two extremes, and everyone has experience of varying degrees of trauma and varying degrees of being able to work through it. But the process of working through a trauma is very similar to the process of working through loss. Loss and bereavement are central to the understanding of human functioning that psychoanalysis has developed since Freud wrote "Mourning and melancholia" (1917e).

Trauma always involves loss and is always life changing. Life is never the same again and this in itself is a loss, a loss of what was. The process of recovering from a loss is that of grieving and this involves a gradual acceptance of the loss and the changes that it has brought, a letting go of the past and a moving on so that one can live in the present and for the future. Both Billy and Monica had the task of recovering from the traumas that had hit them, of reconciling themselves to their losses, accepting the reality of the trauma, and rebuilding their perception of themselves and their world.

There is of course one obvious and important difference between Billy and Monica, and that is that they are very different ages.

Billy is too young to think about his experience with his child-minder that morning, to put it into a context of other experiences, to actively consider how he feels about the way he is treated. His emotional response will be completely unconscious. He may realise the following morning that he does not want to go to the child-minder again, but he is unlikely to know very much about why he does not want to go. If his parents are able to wonder if something has happened to upset him they may be able to reassure him that he is a big boy now and will be able to find a way to fit in and enjoy his time there. This is a way of saying to him that he does have strength of personality and he can use that to make his own place in the group that is the child-minders home in the mornings. What is happening in this case would be that the parents are doing the work of thinking about how Billy feels and what it is that he needs help with, because Billy cannot do this for himself. If this working through on the part of the parents can be taken in by Billy, if he can subconsciously absorb something of their faith in him, and this can mean more to him than his experience of being spoken to harshly, then his sense of himself can be helped to grow. On the other hand if his way of expressing his feelings about his child-minder is to throw his breakfast on the floor, refuse to get dressed, break his toys in the morning, then it may be that he is sent off to his child-minder by angry stressed parents who cannot wonder if something has gone wrong.

This is something of what happened with Roger, a young man who will be discussed in chapter five. His parents, though loving and kind, could not bear to think about emotional pain and could not bear to think about the emotional pain of their children. The result was that Roger was never helped to talk about, to put in context, to have his own unique thoughts about the events in his life that upset him. As a result they remained raw and undigested. This had a massive impact upon his development as an individual because as an adult he had no resources within his own mind to which he could turn to help him to think about his own feelings. His own feelings were perpetually overwhelming for him and he found refuge from pain and confusion by blotting out his mind with drink and drugs. The early traumas of his everyday life and the difficulty of working them through, had a defining impact on Roger's adult life and on his ability to function as an adult.

Many people who have unresolved trauma in their history make huge lifetime decisions on the basis, not so much of the trauma itself but of the unresolved nature of that trauma. Many people who are abused as children grow up to want to work with abused children. They want to care for the lost unloved child in themselves, that they recognise in other children. They want to make something better that has not been made better. Some people who have been expected to be prematurely independent grow up to want to be authority figures such as police or prison officers. They are seeking to create assurance, the security of knowing that someone is in charge.

The decisions that we make as adults are often heavily influenced by the extent to which we have or have not been helped to recover from and to grow from the traumas that we have experienced.

If those traumas are actually inflicted by the very people to whom we have to turn when we are in need (i.e., if we are deliberately hurt and mistreated by our parents) then indeed we are seriously impaired in the task of growing up and finding a rewarding and satisfactory place for ourselves in the world in which we live.

As I suggested earlier, Billy may have had repeated experiences like the one that I witnessed and if no one ever noticed that he was distressed and unhappy these shocks to the system may have built into a sense of himself as someone who did not know how to get things right. Trauma and how we deal with it, has an impact upon how we experience ourselves and the decisions that we make.

Monica faced a different task in working through the trauma of "9/11". Her world and her sense of self had been well established prior to this trauma. She was not still developing as a personality, she was moving through her adult life, working, raising a family. Jack did survive the events of the collapse of the World Trade Centre, but he was a different man afterwards. He had been unable to save lives, but had found dead bodies, and parts of bodies. He had thrown himself into the rescue effort and into the ongoing work of trying to find people, but he experienced more failure than success in this attempt and even though it was not his fault, he felt that he had let people down by not rescuing them alive. He was ultimately a broken man who suffered nightmares, depression, flashbacks. He went from seeing himself as a strong member of an admired profession, to seeing himself as a miserable wreck of a man. He was not the man that Monica had woken up with on the morning of 9/11. He did find help and he did gradually and over a long period of time, remember, and work through the events of that day and the subsequent weeks and months. But he never regained his previous sense of self confidence and he didn't think of himself as a hero. Being a firefighter had been his way of feeling that he was a real masculine man, and actually this was in itself something of a defence mechanism as it masked an underlying repressed anxiety about his intellectual strength. As a child he had felt humiliated in school when he had not been able to learn his lessons as quickly as other children.

The events of 9/11 robbed him of this defence mechanism and he felt broken.

There are many examples of trauma, shocks that bring us to a full stop, that for a moment or for longer, overwhelm our thinking and prevent us from carrying on with our everyday tasks. Billy and Monica are at either end of a large spectrum of experience of trauma. It always involves loss and change and it changes not only the external world but perhaps more importantly, the world of the mind, our internal world.

How we deal with trauma and how we are enabled to deal with trauma emotionally, will have a big impact upon how well we recover from it. The extent to which we can recover from it will have an impact upon whether we need to put in place defence mechanisms to protect ourselves from the raw and unprocessed experience of the trauma, or whether we become able to remember it and think about the feelings associated with it in a thoughtful manner.

Roger was not able to think at all, he desperately sought escape from the panic inside his own mind. Someone else might carry great anger and rage inside themselves which may get expressed as violence and aggression. Another person may sink into depression without really knowing why. In either case the emotional experience is one of having lost the ability to use one's mind to begin to psychologically resolve a situation, and of having to recover one's own mind in a somewhat different way.

Many people can use their relationships with others to help them to recover from trauma. I know someone who has suffered repeated sudden and unexpected losses of loved ones throughout her life, but she has always had loving understanding family and friends to turn to and she has been able to use their care to support her through a collapsed state and to help her find her strength again. Her attitude to life is to make the most of everyday because life is a good and precious gift to be valued and enjoyed.

To summarise, psychological trauma is an event that breaks through our protective emotional skin and causes a wound. The feelings are of being completely overwhelmed by an event and unable to function. The world, our own world, is for a time a place that we do not recognise and do not understand. We are lost, we no longer know what is real and what is not. This sudden unexpected assault on our psyche brings us to a halt and for a time we are unable to function. Gradually we move on from the event itself. This moving on can be reparative and can involve personal growth and strength, or the trauma can become an event around which defence mechanisms are put in place in order to push away or deny the pain of the trauma.

Whether the trauma leads to emotional growth or emotional constriction will depend on the psychological resources of the individual and on the help that they do or do not receive, in the task of processing the trauma. If the trauma has been caused, perhaps deliberately, and is repeated, as in ongoing abuse, then the person, especially a child, has little opportunity to work through the way in which they are treated and is likely to develop and to utilize defence mechanisms to an extreme degree in an attempt to shut out the pain and humiliation of the trauma to which they are subjected. Such a child is likely to grow up into an adult who does not have a capacity to function effectively in the ordinary community.

On the other hand everyone experiences trauma to a greater or lesser degree and if we can be helped to process those traumas and to think about them, we can use them as experiences from which we can develop resilience and strength, and this will support us through the ongoing conflicts and difficulties that arise throughout the life cycle.

THREE

Anxiety

What is anxiety all about? Why do people worry so much? Does it serve a purpose in some obscure way? Is there a point to being stressed?

Mental health difficulties generally are on the increase. More and more people are going to their GP and saying "I just can't cope anymore". More and more people are taking time off work with stress, more and more people are being diagnosed with depression or anxiety or both. Hearing someone say that they feel stressed or they are going through a very stressful time is not unusual.

It seems that anxiety, stress, excessive worrying, has become a big aspect of the daily lives of a large proportion of the ordinary men and women, and indeed children, of the affluent Western world. The causes of stress and anxiety are almost always attributed to modern life being difficult. Finding a good job can be hard, having enough money, finding a decent place to live; many aspects of everyday life seem to be fraught with anxiety. And it is often thought that if some aspect of life could be altered, the anxiety would go away. If we could win the lottery, or find the perfect job, all the anxiety would just disappear, we would no longer have anything to worry about.

But is it just about having the ideal life, or does our own individual psychological and unconscious world also have something to contribute to the reasons for anxiety? I like to think that it does, not least because if it does we have a chance of working through our own internal issues and this could lead to a lowering of anxiety and a greater freedom to find more satisfaction in the job, house, money, and relationships that we do have. There are very real pressures for many people, but how these real, or sometimes imagined, pressures interact with the unconscious aspects of our own personality, will play a large part in how those pressures impact upon our state of mind.

I suppose what I am trying to say here is that some people seem to have a capacity to enjoy life to the full, and others are beset by an attitude of doom and gloom. Their situations may be very similar but their attitudes are different, and it is this that makes all the difference to their quality of life.

Where to begin? Like all aspects of human emotional life it is complicated. In this chapter I hope to address the subject with some simplicity, and, of course, to do so from a psychoanalytic perspective.

This chapter on anxiety will be followed by the chapter on defence mechanisms because anxiety can itself be thought of as a defensive response to danger. It can be thought of as a bodily warning sign that something is wrong. The heart rate increases, a state of tension is felt in one's muscles, one becomes alert and on edge, and all these signs tell us that something is not right. We feel anxious when something is not right, and the more anxious we feel, the more not right things seem to be.

If we are crossing the road and see a car travelling towards us at speed, we automatically recognise this as a dangerous situation and run. It is as though our body acts before our mind has even realised what we are doing. It is when we reach the safety of the pavement that we become aware of the emotional impact of the moment of danger. We may feel shocked, we may feel angry with the driver or humiliated by our own sense of vulnerability. But what we have experienced is a moment of knowing that we are in danger, with all the accompanying physical responses to that. That moment of knowing can be termed fear or anxiety, or stress. All these words express an emotional state of mind that is on the spectrum of anxiety, from extreme fear at one end, to a mild sense of concern at the other.

Freud wrote two important papers to do with anxiety. The first was called "Anxiety" (1916) and is included in his volume, *Introductory Lectures on Psychoanalysis* (1916–17). The second is entitled *Inhibitions, Symptoms and Anxiety* (1926d [1925]).

In these two papers he raises the question of anxiety and attempts to track down its root cause.

He begins by asserting that there is a difference between realistic anxiety and neurotic anxiety. In the instance given above of a car approaching at speed, it could be argued that an anxiety response is realistic because there is a real danger that needs to be responded to and it is the feeling of anxiety that alerts a person to the need to act.

The action is likely to be a choice between what has become popularly known as fight or flight (Cannon, 1932). In other words the choice is a rather primitive one of running away from danger or standing one's ground and fighting off the danger. In the instance of an approaching car it would make sense to flee rather than to assert one's right to cross the road at a pace of one's own choosing. On the other hand if someone is attempting to steal your handbag or your purse you may be more inclined to fight the person off rather than just run away. These responses are familiar to us and it is possible to understand how we might react spontaneously to such danger situations without having time to think through strategies, or to actually be aware of feeling anxiety until later.

But what might be more of a problem, and also perhaps more interesting, is the situation of anxiety occurring when there is no realistic danger.

This is what Freud (1926d [1925]) referred to as a "neurotic" anxiety. This also takes us closer to the realm of phobic anxiety. For example many people become anxious when they see a spider. Some people become very anxious in enclosed spaces like elevators. Others become anxious in spaces that are too open. In these instances there is not necessarily a real danger and what is interesting is that a phobia of spiders is not linked to the actuality of their being in any way dangerous, or threatening. People in countries that do not have dangerous spiders are nevertheless scared of them. Some people cannot go into a room if they think that there may be a spider in that room. I know of someone who lives in England where we do not usually have dangerous spiders, and has never been hurt by a spider. She cannot rationally explain her revulsion, but she cannot bear to think that she is anywhere near one and will shrink away and become distressed if she sees one. In fact she does not even have to see or be told that there is a spider in the room to become distressed, this will happen if someone just mentions them. There is nothing rational or realistic in this situation, which is nevertheless fraught with anxiety, bordering on fear. The question of how to make sense of anxiety that is essentially senseless, is complex.

Freud and subsequent psychoanalytic thinkers, are interested to trace this type of anxiety back to its original roots. He thought that the first experience of danger, and therefore of anxiety, was birth. Being born is a dangerous event, and in Freud's day was very much more dangerous than it is in the Western world today. Many babies and mothers died during childbirth, and many babies underwent a birth that left them damaged in some way. But it was actually the separation from the mother that Freud considered to be the first anxiety situation. He qualified this by pointing to the distress that a very young baby can express when they are expecting to see their mother and in fact it is another person whose face comes into view. Anyone who has babysat for a baby who has awoken whilst the mother is out will know this experience. The baby will be quite happy whilst they think that it will be their mother who will come to the cot to pick them up, but will quickly cry when someone they do not know well actually comes into the room and takes them out. Freud considered that this awareness of separation created anxiety, but he also thought that it was the result of what we might call disappointment. The infant is longing to see the mother's face and when that longing is denied satisfaction, a state of anxiety is formed.

In itself this does not quite add up. Why should it be anxiety that is the response to a denied satisfaction, why not perhaps, anger, or sorrow, or just disappointment?

We need to turn to the work of Melanie Klein (1921–1945) for some help with this question. She thought that anxiety was not simply to do with being without the longed for person, but to do with being *with* something inside oneself which is potentially dangerous. In other words, the infant who cannot have the desired object/mother, is not just without something, they are left with a whole range of feelings that they may not be able to manage. One of these may be anxiety about where the mother has gone, is she coming back, why has she left the baby, how dare she leave. The baby may feel unsafe even though in fact they are being well cared for. If they also feel angry, and refuse the care of another person, or do not want their mother when she returns, they may then begin to experience themselves as nasty, vengeful, and destructive of that which they actually do need. In this instance it can be argued that anxiety is a response to an internal threat, and not solely a response to an external threat.

It may be more difficult to admit that we experience ourselves as dangerous, than it is to admit that some external object is threatening, hence we may attribute our anxiety to the presence of an external object such as a spider, or a stranger. After all we can get rid of a spider, but we cannot easily get rid of ourselves, our thoughts, our wishes. The internal state of mind which might feel dangerous may be one of destructive rage, either towards another or towards oneself, and Melanie Klein, again, distinguished between fear to do with the safety of oneself and fear to do with the safety of others. She called these "persecutory anxieties" (1934 [1921–1945]) and "depressive anxieties" (1946).

PERSECUTORY ANXIETIES

This, as the term suggests, is to do with the sense of being under attack by something external. The person who believes that a spider will do them some harm could be said to be suffering from persecutory anxiety. As an example this is very simple and in actuality persecutory anxiety can be much more complex and difficult to track down to its roots. However Freud (1909b) offered us a good example of such an attempt in his paper "Analysis of a phobia in a five year old boy" more popularly known as "Little Hans".

Little Hans was a five-year-old boy who developed a fear of horses. His father wrote to Freud to tell him about his son's fears and the two men had a correspondence in which Freud attempted to assist the father in helping his little boy to overcome his fear. It is a long paper and worth reading, but to summarise, Little Hans had developed a fear of horses after seeing a horse falling in the street outside his house. His fear became so great that he began to refuse to leave his house. His parents noted that at around the same time as this fear developed Hans had become aware of, and very interested in, his penis, which he called his widdler. His mother had told him that if he played with his widdler the doctor would come and chop it off. He had had some anxiety dreams about losing his mother.

It would have been the case in 1909 that horses were plentiful in the streets of town, cities, and in the countryside. It would also have been the case that they could represent a real danger, especially if they were out of control as indeed a horse that is falling down would be. So there is a sense in which Little Hans had witnessed a scene which was actually dangerous and his anxiety could be thought to be realistic.

But it developed into a phobia that was not modified by the reassurance of the people who had always kept him safe, his parents.

They had thought that the development of a phobia was linked to his awareness of, and interest in, his widdler. Before Freud had said anything, they had sensed that their son's level of anxiety was being focused on horses but was actually to do with something much closer to home.

The sense that a person's named anxiety is not the real anxiety is common. We have probably all noticed this not only in other people but also in ourselves.

To cut a long story short, Freud declared that Little Hans was suffering with castration anxiety, a fear that his highly valued and very important penis would be lost to him, taken away as threatened. He was so anxious about this that he could not acknowledge it directly but displaced his anxiety onto something else that was perceived to be a suitable substitute for his castration anxiety.

It was thought that his anxiety was further compounded by his love for his mother, who had been the one to articulate the possibility of losing his penis, and his worry that in loving his mother he may offend his father, who he also loved.

This is a very truncated version of the case history, and it does deserve a good deal more space and thoughtful consideration than I wish to give in this particular context.

But what I hope I can show by this account is something of how complicated feelings of love, desire, and competition can give rise to an anxiety that is fundamentally to do with loss of something valued.

I think it is fair to suggest that a man's penis is not only valued by him, but is also the symbol of his maleness and therefore intrinsically bound up with his sense of identity, potency, and of course sexuality.

It is also a very common experience for boys to be threatened with the loss of it if they play with it too much.

This makes it seem as if such an anxiety may be an exclusively male experience, but females can also be threatened with the loss of an aspect of themselves that is felt to be very precious and symbolic of their identity as women and as valuable members of their family and cultural and work place groups. This does not have to be a physical part of them, though it may be, but it can be to do with their capacity to think, to contribute, to be creative. In other words something not so easily noticed as a penis but just as important in a more subtle and diffuse sense.

But the other important point to take from the story of Little Hans is that as the attempt to understand his phobia was traced to its origin, it became linked to his desire and longing for something, and his fear that it was the very fact that he had such longings that led to the possibility of losing the longed for object.

This is at the heart of the emotional experience that we call anxiety, the dread of the loss of that which is loved and desired, and that we fear we will cause the loss of it through our aggressive attempts to take possession of it. These feelings are focused upon actual things or people but are actually to do with a loss of self, or an aspect of self or identity.

If we trace his phobia from the other direction we can hypothesise that Little Hans loved and desired his mother. He was concerned that his love and desire for his mother would displease his father, that there would be competition between them. Hans also loved his father, so this formed one internal, and unconscious conflict. His mother had made clear her disapproval of his playing with his widdler and threatened him with the loss of it, which he did not want. But he did want to play with it. Here was another conflict. He had longings and desires for which he feared he may be punished.

Then as it happened he witnessed the horse falling down and being injured. It seemed to Hans that his unconscious fantasy had been played out, the horse was suffering what Hans was afraid of suffering, and came to represent in Hans' imagination, the object of terror, the focus of anxiety. Little Hans suffered persecutory anxiety at the thought of going out of the house and encountering a horse.

Just to sum it up again, we can say that persecutory anxiety is to do with the fear of losing something valued and precious, and that this results from our own aggressive desire and longing for that loved precious object.

DEPRESSIVE ANXIETY

Klein took this thinking further and discussed what she called depressive anxiety. This was to do with the fear of not being good enough for the loved object, and the ambivalence that is involved in feeling both love and hate towards someone. Although we might term Hans' anxiety as persecutory because he is fearful of attack, we could also say that he is in a conflict of love and hate because whilst he loves his mother very much, he also hates the fact that he has been threatened with castration if he plays with his widdler. Whilst he loves his father very much, he also hates the fact that his father can lay claim to an exclusive relationship with Hans' mother. It is only conceptually that one would separate these two forms of anxiety as experientially the fear of our hatred destroying that which we value would be likely to be intrinsically linked with the worry of not being adequate for the object. Take an example of a mother who is worried about being able to care for her new baby properly. This is a very common fear amongst new mothers. What they are really saying is that they are anxious that they will not be able to meet the needs of their infant. This may be couched in terms of feeding or nappy changing, but at a more unconscious level it is likely to be to do with being able to love fully, and nurture the relationship. They may be fearful that they will harm with their attempt to love the infant. If this were to happen, then the longed for loving relationship might be lost. Dislike, conflict, and even hatred might dominate the relationship rather than love and care.

Once again the worry gets focused onto something external, but is actually to do with an unconscious and internal state of affairs in which aggressive, destructive fantasies are having to be managed and subdued.

In my own work place of a university setting, we have recently been going through a radical reorganisation of the departments and the administrative and academic staff. Anyone who has been involved in an organisational restructuring will know just how stressful and anxiety provoking this can be. During the course of this I was on my way into work one day and was thinking that I did not want to be there because I did not want to have to spend the day in such a stressful atmosphere. At a conscious level I was worried about an external impact upon my mental equilibrium. Then I realised that I was having a fleeting fantasy of it all getting too much for me and that I would in moment of rage, just announce that I was leaving. It seemed to me, on reflection, that whilst I was not looking forward to my day at work, what was really bothering me was that I would not be able to control my own irrational aggression, and that this would lead me to take an aggressive action that would result in me leaving my job, which I actually value very much. When I could think that I might be more frightened of myself than of my environment, I was able to get a more rational perspective on the day ahead, and whilst I still did not anticipate having a great day, I did feel that I could manage it without being destructive, and hold on to a sense that in due course this time of uncertainty would come to an end. I finally arrived at my office feeling less anxious and more sanguine about the day ahead. What is equally important is that having done a little bit of internal work in my own mind, I was then freer to enjoy what was enjoyable about the day and to be more fully engaged in my tasks, which ultimately was much more satisfying than feeling anxiously resentful all day.

In a way I moved from what could be termed persecutory anxiety, to what could be termed depressive anxiety. To begin with I felt attacked by the plans for reorganisation, that these plans would hurt me in some way and I would be harmed by them – persecutory anxiety. But as I reflected on my own state of mind I became aware of a sense of not being able to cope and that I was not up to the task of surviving the reorganisation, or dealing with the new changes and challenges that this would bring – depressive anxiety. This then led to a fantasy of handing in my notice, which would mean that I did not have to face the anxiety provoking situation at all, much like Little Hans resolved to not leave the house so as to not see the horses that provoked his fears. However if I did hand in my notice I would deal with that threat, but at the expense of losing something much bigger and more valuable, my job. Similarly Little Hans was in danger of losing his freedom to go out into the street by his attempt to resolve his anxieties by focusing them upon the horses.

When a person's anxiety reaches such pitch that they feel unable to go to work, or they cannot enter a room in case there is a spider there, or they cannot use the elevator in a high story building, their lives have become dominated by irrational thinking, but it is their way of attempting to resolve an emotional dilemma that they do not understand and cannot find a way of thinking through so that the fear loses its grip upon them.

This is an important point in any form of mental health difficulty: the symptoms that are seen from the outside to be the problem, are, for the person, their way of attempting to resolve a much deeper, more unconscious, and more distressing problem. This again is something that Freud (1924b) first pointed out when he was thinking about severe mental health difficulties that we would now call personality disorder. He concluded that for the patient the symptoms are the attempt to cure the disease, they are not the disease itself.

The parents of Little Hans could have taken his symptoms at face value and addressed his fear of horses by trying to coax him into seeing them as non-frightening. They could have tried to get him to gradually be near them, and then maybe to touch them. In this way he may have been able to reduce his overwhelming fear of horses and been able to go out into the street again. But they would not have helped him with the internal fears of his own destructiveness that gave rise to the phobia, and the underlying distress would have gone unnoticed and possibly un-remedied.

Similarly, had I left my job when I felt that I did not want to go to work that day, I would have found a solution for the symptoms but not for the underlying fears of my own impulses to act in a way that was destructive to myself, and then probably to others, my colleagues, my family, etc.

One of the reasons that we look for a focus for anxiety can be that it is so awful to feel that the cause is unknown. We feel even worse if we are unable to make any sense of a situation, and so we try to make sense of our fears by attributing them to something like the presence of a spider, or an enclosed space. When we feel overwhelming anxiety and cannot attribute it to anything it does feel intolerable as we are left with a sense of dread. We then feel that we are in the grip of this dread. If we can attribute the feeling to an external event we can feel that we have at least got some kind of handle on the feelings and that we might be able to get some measure of control back, over ourselves and our mental state. This is why solitary confinement becomes such a torture if it is continued for any length of time. People who are kept in solitary confinement are being forced to be alone with themselves, with their own fears and fantasies. This is what Melanie Klein was talking about in relation to the infant who is left alone for too long. It is not that they are without anyone but that they are with the contents of their own mind, and their own mind is full of terrifying ideas and images. Neither babies nor adults can tolerate this for very long and it is indeed a wretched cruelty to subject a person to such a situation for any length of time. When a despotic political regime wishes to subject a person to intolerable cruelty, they leave that person with nothing but themselves, knowing that this will drive the person mad with despair and the terror of their own imagination.

It is not the spider in the room that terrifies, it is the thoughts and unconscious imaginings that become located in spiders. Spiders do have a tendency to appear unannounced and to scuttle across the room, only seen from the corner of one's eye. Thus is can be with unwelcome thoughts and desires, and thus the spider can become a useful focus for the fear of such unwanted thoughts and desires.

Anxiety, fears, worries, stress; these are all terms for an emotional state that we all experience every day. If we miss the bus for work in the morning we will feel anxious about being late for work. If we do not complete a task at work we may feel anxious about our employer's opinion of us. If we let down a friend or family member in some way we will be concerned about how they will feel about us.

We feel anxious when we perceive a danger of some sort, a threat to our well-being. We become alerted to a need to take action, to run away or to fight our corner.

We feel anxious when we sense a threat to ourselves or others, and when we sense that we are not capable of carrying out a task that is required of us. This can be called "realistic" anxiety.

Very often these feelings are dissipated by reassurance. We may discover that our boss is willing to give us a second chance, or our friend understands why we let them down. We can feel reassured by the experience of discovering that we can carry out a difficult task and manage it. In these instances we feel anxious, but the feeling is dissolved and altered into something else by experience.

For instance a friend was telling me about her daughter who went into work one day to find a message telling her to report to the senior manager's office as soon as she arrived. She immediately thought that she had done something wrong and that the meeting would involve her being reprimanded and possibly sacked.

When she got into the meeting she discovered that in fact her opinion was being sought about some difficulties within her team between other people. She was actually perceived as having an ability to take a balanced view of situations and to be the person most likely to give a true picture of the personalities involved. She did this and the end result was not at all anxiety but the opposite. She gained confidence and self-esteem, and realised that she could assume that her opinions would carry a certain authority in that setting.

But when a state of anxiety becomes established, or irrational or phobic, this is what was once thought of as "neurotic" anxiety. This has been further divided into persecutory anxiety, a threat from outside to oneself, or depressive anxiety, a threat to another that results from one's own shortcomings.

In either case it is possible to see that the focus of the anxiety is not the problem, but is in some way, representative of the problem. The problem that gives rise to the anxiety is usually to do with a fear of one's own unconscious aggressive drives that threaten to destroy that which we love most.

We are never so afraid of anything as much as we are of our own destructive feelings and impulses.

When we hear through the media of an unprovoked and murderous attack on an apparently innocent person, we are hearing about someone whose behaviour is dominated by unthinking aggression and hatred. We are rightly frightened by such people, but we are also frightened by such feelings in ourselves and we need to know that we can control them. For some people the confusion of such primitive feelings is huge and one way of trying to manage them is to develop symptoms that both express the real problem and deflect from it.

This is when anxiety becomes a dominating constraint in a person's life.

FOUR

Defence mechanisms

In Chapter Two we looked at two ways of thinking about the structure of the mind. One of these is as an entity that has both conscious and unconscious aspects, the topographical model. The other is the structural model, which is contained within the topographical model and in which the mind is thought of as having three basic aspects that interact with each other and are involved in the everyday decisions and choices that we make. These three aspects are the id, the ego, and the superego.

When Sigmund Freud first conceived of the these models he thought that the unconscious aspect of the mind contained memories, thoughts, and fantasies that had been shut away from awareness because the conscious aspect of the mind did not wish to know about them, or could not bear the emotional pain of knowing or remembering. The term that he gave to this process of pushing away painful thoughts, feelings and memories, is "repression".

Repression was the formulation around which defence mechanisms were first conceptualised.

Defence mechanisms are the unconscious psychological systems that we put in place in order to protect ourselves from emotional pain, and from anxiety. From the moment we are born we are seeking to ensure that we feel safe and contented. Such safety and contentment may be well facilitated by those who care for us, or it may be poorly facilitated, we may even be mistreated as opposed to being cared for. Our early experiences of being able to feel reliably safe, warm, and free from pain or discomfort, will have a huge impact on how we think of the world around us, and how we attempt to organise our minds in order to ensure that we do not have to endure intolerable emotional pain.

Once again it was Sigmund Freud, (1917 [1916–1917]) who first thought about and wrote about the ordinary ways in which people attempt to deal with feelings that are difficult. He suggested that we have all put in place unconscious psychological mechanisms, the purpose of which is to protect us from emotional pain. These are what we call defence mechanisms. They are in a sense coping strategies, except that they are unconscious and they tend to become established aspects of our personality as we develop from infancy to adulthood.

It is not just emotional pain that we need to defend against, we also have to find ways of coping with anxiety. Anxiety can be thought of as the worrying anticipation of emotional pain. If we know that we have to face a situation that we have previously found painful we may well begin to feel the stress of that situation before we actually get to it. We begin to suffer some time before the pain actually happens. Sometimes just thinking about the prospect of suffering can make us feel unwell and distressed.

This chapter will look at a number of defence mechanisms one at a time. Freud's daughter Anna, took forward her father's work in this area, identifying five categories of defence mechanisms to which she gave the terms; repression, reaction formation, regression, sublimation. This chapter will also discuss denial and displacement. Emotional pain and anxiety will be considered in the context of each type of defence mechanism.

Repression was the first form of a defence mechanism that Freud identified. He said (Freud, 1914d, p. 16) *the theory of repression is the cornerstone on which the whole structure of psychoanalysis rests.*

In her paper "The defences", Galatariotou (2005, p. 19) states "Repression is the foundation of the unconscious and the exploration of the unconscious is the central characteristic of psychoanalysis."

The Oxford English dictionary defines the word repress as "To actively exclude (an unwanted thought) from conscious awareness."

It is an unconscious process of pushing away, pushing down any awareness of unwanted thoughts or feelings. It is a way of persuading ourselves that we do not have a particular thought or a feeling. It is a feature of psychological life that is probably easier to observe in others than in ourselves.

For example, I used to know someone who always forgot his wife's birthday. The background situation and the history of their relationship, was complicated but in this one respect he simply forgot or repressed his awareness of the fact that her birthday was approaching or had arrived. She in turn repressed any hurt that she felt about this, saying that she did not care about her birthday anyway. In this way they both agreed to ignore her birthday by repressing any awareness of it as a significant event in the year. This repression was a small aspect of the overall picture, but serves as an example of how repression works.

We can think of political repression as being a similar process but on a larger societal scale. There is a view, an opinion, a criticism of a regime that is unacceptable to that regime and must be stifled, because it is considered to be a destabilising opinion. It cannot be discussed or debated, it must be buried and pushed out of awareness. There are political regimes that lock away, or even assassinate, anyone who voices dissent so that the voice cannot be heard. We call this repression and we all do this to ourselves when a thought, a response, a wish is felt to be too difficult, too unacceptable, to be allowed into consciousness.

But repressed thoughts and wishes do not go away altogether. They have a habit of returning so that we have to tackle them all over again and seek to create more effective ways of dealing with them. Simple repression may work for simple or not very important wishes but more urgent and pressing demands will re-emerge in some way at some time. This process is often referred to as *the return of the repressed* (Freud, 1896b). The return of the repressed is to do with the many ways in which repressed desires get expressed or make themselves known, in spite of the ego's attempts to deny their existence, through inadvertent references, slips of the tongue, or the development of further symptoms and mental health difficulties, such as obsessions and phobias.

An obsessional person may have repressed their own messy self by trying to be fastidiously clean, but of course in being overly concerned with keeping everything very clean, they are actually constantly having to ward off the messiness. It doesn't go away, it is very present and a big part of their lives. The very thing that they are attempting to disown, is a constant companion in their daily lives. That which they wished to repress, has returned with increased power over them.

Some wishes and desires will be demanding enough, and unacceptable enough to require more determined efforts on the part of our superegos, to become effectively denied.

One such effort may result in what is called "reaction formation".

Reaction formation is a term used to describe a way of being that is quite contrary to the way that we really feel.

One can see this in small ways in many situations in everyday life. The little boy who falls over in the playground and hurts his leg, and then with tears of humiliation in his eyes smiles and laughs along with his friends who are also laughing at him. This is reaction formation, he is persuading himself that what he feels is the opposite of what he really feels.

In thinking about this I am reminded of the woman who I introduced in chapter one, who is very passive and compliant in her presentation and who is always fearful of being wrong. She does not sleep well. It is not clear why she does not sleep but one reason seems to be that she is frightened of dreaming because when she does sleep and dream her dreams are actually full of violent destruction. Her unconscious world is quite the opposite of her conscious thinking, and of her presentation of herself to others around her. To others she presents as someone compliant, sweet, and eager to please. In the privacy of her unconscious she is full of hatred, violence, and destruction. In her conscious waking life she is dominated by her superego, but at night in her unconscious dreaming mind, she is dominated by her id. She has reacted to her violent destructive feelings by forming a persona that is very different and in doing so has persuaded herself and others that she is a sweet natured person when in fact her personality contains a great deal that is not at all sweet.

When we have unacceptable thoughts or feelings, we have to push them away, do something else with them. We can repress them or we can turn them around, reaction formation. It is necessary that we do this or we would simply punch everyone who annoys us, or steal things rather than bother to pay for them. Repression is a necessary defence mechanism, but like all defence mechanisms it can be taken to extremes and can become an established aspect of personality that serves to obscure and distort the awareness of the real personality rather than to express it.

There are characters in the classic children's story *The Wonderful Wizard of Oz* (1900), by L. Frank Baum, who can be thought of as having in place a reaction formation defence mechanism.

Without going into too much detail, *The Wonderful Wizard of Oz* is the story of a journey undertaken by a young girl, Dorothy. She is accompanied on this journey by three characters, the tin man, who has no heart, the lion without a roar, and the scarecrow with no brain. In the course of their adventures together, they all discover their missing aspects of self. The tin man discovers that he does have a heart and feelings, the lion does develop a roar and learn to stand up for himself and the scarecrow finds his brain and can think. They could be thought about as having previously pushed out of awareness those aspects of themselves, through the use of the defence of reaction formation. They have developed a way of being that is the opposite of who they really are. During the course of their adventures they recover those aspects of thoughts and feelings and can integrate them into their personalities. In this way they can become more fully themselves.

Outside of story books we may encounter people who are extremely clean and tidy, which may be a reaction to some very grubby messy thoughts and feelings, or someone who is very shy, which may be a response to fantasies of showing off.

REGRESSION

A return to a former or less developed state.

The task of growing up, of becoming a mature adult, has many difficulties and hurdles for everyone. Whilst we all share some of these, we also have our own particular difficulties that are not quite the same as anyone else's. When we encounter these difficulties, a part of us may prefer to not have to grow up anymore, to be able to stay childlike and not take on the challenge of the next aspect of development. Eventually we all become adults and then find that there are times when being an adult feels as though it is more than we can tolerate, we would prefer to be able to regress back to a childlike state of being, in which we do not have to manage adult responsibilities.

A common experience that many of us have is that of not wanting to get out of bed in the morning, we are cosy and warm where we are and the thought of getting up, maybe when it is cold and dark is not welcome. One thought or feeling might be that we feel unwell and therefore unable to go to work or college. When we are unwell we feel unable to function in our usual way, we need to be allowed to put aside our usual responsibilities and to have others take care of us. We become again rather like dependent children who need care and protection. This is an example of a return to a former or less developed state and can be thought of a regressive state of mind.

When we cannot cope with the demands and responsibilities of adult life, we might regress to an earlier stage of development and become childlike. This might be an unconscious attempt to become someone who does not have to behave in an adult way, and thus is excused from doing so.

If we are ill, we need to regress in order to recover. We may need to be cared for by others, or we may just need to be allowed to relinquish our daily responsibilities and stay at home.

I heard a story about a four-year-old boy who had a temper tantrum at the end of a long and exciting day. It could be said that he regressed at that point to a baby like state, but actually he was still at an age at which temper tantrums are common, so perhaps he had not so much regressed, as not progressed to a more mature level of functioning. However, had his mother, in response to his tantrum, thrown herself on the floor and cried and wailed, we would definitely be justified in considering that she had regressed to an infantile level of functioning, as a way of coping with a situation that felt overwhelming for her at that point.

People regress several times a day in small ways. We get home from work, throw off our shoes, curl up on the sofa and want a drink. In childhood that might have been a glass of milk and a biscuit, in adulthood it might be an alcoholic drink. We feel that having behaved in a mature adult way all day, we now deserve to be more self-indulgent, to unwind. This is a small example of regression, but when it becomes a defence mechanism it can be more of a way of life and can indicate real difficulties with functioning in the world of adult relationships.

Someone who drinks instead of going to work, is perhaps in a regressed state of mind. A student who cannot work, cannot produce the essays that they need to produce, feels stuck, and may be in a regressed state of mind. They may have retreated to a psychological position in which they feel too small and helpless to carry out their adult tasks.

The superego aspect of their mind that plays a part in self-discipline, is not functioning, or if it is over functioning, the ego is not able to negotiate between the two and find an acceptable compromise.

Parents have to make many daily decisions about how to balance compassion with discipline with their children. Sometimes they have to repress their anger and aggression towards them and sometimes they have to be more firm than they might like to be. They are not necessarily repressing their feelings in this instance but may be channelling their intuitive responses in a more considered direction. For example instead of shouting at a child who has just broken a plate or a cup, the child may be required to do some helpful things around the house in order to make amends. The parent may feel absolutely exasperated, but choose not to express this in an unrestrained way. They may wish that they could become regressed for a while but may have enough ego strength to think through the situation and make a more considered decision.

This leads us to the last defence mechanism that Anna Freud identified that of sublimation.

Sublimation is to do with using thoughts, feelings, wishes, that are not acceptable in their original form, as the motivating factor in the creation of something useful and beneficial. We probably all have some curiosity about the insides of the human body. This is something that is very important to us, but cannot be readily investigated. It could be suggested, and it may be true in some cases, that someone who chooses to become a surgeon in adult life, is sublimating a powerful wish to know the inside of the human body. By becoming a surgeon she is able to gratify this wish in a way that is valuable and appreciated by the person and by society in general, and this is considered to be much better than simply opening up bodies out of curiosity.

Some police officers are afraid of their own attraction to criminality, but if they focus that fascination into the resolving of crimes, it can be thought to have been well sublimated. In this instance it is hardly a defence mechanism as it has been converted to a more productive purpose, but it is in part, a response to something unacceptable within the self.

We can see from this discussion that people have to make daily decisions about how to manage their unacceptable thoughts, wishes, and feelings. When we wake up in the morning and do not want to get up we may begin by trying to repress the thought that it is time to get up. We may try to pretend that it is not really seven a.m. and try to go back to sleep. Then we may regress by wondering if we feel ill and need to have a day off. We may begin to persuade ourselves that we feel rather poorly to do a day's work, and may be thinking of telling people this, so that we can invite sympathy and offers of care. We may then have to realise that we do have to get up and get dressed and go to work, so we might at that point begin to tell ourselves that actually we hate being in bed and we really want to get up and get moving straight away. This might get us out of bed in the first instance, but we will need more than a bit of reaction formation to support us through the day, so we will then look to sublimate our desire to be regressed by finding something to which we can look forward during our day. This may be a particularly enjoyable aspect of our job, or knowing that we will see people that we like and respect. We might then feel able to work in the knowledge that this will give us more satisfaction and a greater sense of well-being, than staying in bed all day pretending to be ill. This would be called sublimation.

The artist may make good creative use of their own internal conflicts and difficulties to produce a magnificent painting. The painting "The scream" by Edvard Munch, 1893, is perhaps a very powerful example of this, but many creative projects are born of frustration and a need to work through internal emotional struggles, a need to express primitive thoughts and feelings in a creative and productive form.

DENIAL AND DISPLACEMENT

All of the above are labels given to some of the different ways in which we seek to protect ourselves against real or imagined attacks on our sense of well-being, whether these attacks come from within ourselves or are thought to come from elsewhere.

There are two terms in more common use that Anna Freud (1936) also used and developed, and these are denial and displacement.

Denial is used to describe the psychological mechanism of refusing to believe something that is actually the truth. We say that someone is in denial when they insist that an unwelcome, and to them unbearable situation, does not really exist or they insist that it has not happened. Denial is commonly seen in people who are alcoholic for example. It is not unusual for people who are alcohol dependent to insist that they do not drink or that they can give it up tomorrow without any trouble. They pretend to themselves that their drinking is within normal limits and that they are in control when everyone else can see that they actually have a serious problem with it. They cannot face the truth about their own state of mind. Other addictive behaviour can be thought about in this way also, smoking is another example. Smoking is less common now but for a long time many people smoked and denied the fact that they were seriously increasing their risk of developing lung cancer. Nowadays many young people take drugs and believe that they will do them no harm. Sometimes they do not suffer any ill effect and this encourages an omnipotent denial of the fact that drugs can be harmful.

This denial is different from repression, regression or reaction formation in that it is to do with a determined attempt on the part of the unconscious mind to change the truth, to insist that a situation is not as it is. It can be an aspect of the symptomatology of mental health difficulties and illness. A person may do something and then later be absolutely convinced that they did not do it and insist that it was not them. An extreme example of this would be a young man who was severely mentally unwell who did in fact murder somebody, but then insisted that he did not do so even though the evidence was overwhelming. He had obliterated the truth from his mind and was convinced that he had not committed the murder. The truth is a cause for such mental anguish that it has to be denied, be made to be not the truth.

The last mechanism in this particular list is that of displacement. Again it is a very common defence mechanism employed by all of us at some time and is to do with displacing our feelings about one thing onto another. If we have had a difficult day at work we may be bad tempered at home in the evening. We might snap at a friend when we are actually feeling angry with someone else. We have taken our feelings towards one situation or person and expressed them towards another, placed them elsewhere. Strictly speaking, for this to come under the umbrella of a defence mechanism, it would be an unconscious displacement of feelings, but of course sometimes we can be aware of what we are doing. If we shout at our partner and they point out that they haven't done anything to deserve that, then we may realise that we have displaced our aggression towards someone else on to our partner. In this event our conscious mind would be able to perceive that we had acted unconsciously. We may even have an awareness of what we are doing at the time, but in technical terms the label defence mechanism would indicate a lack of conscious awareness of the mechanism behind the behaviour.

Throughout our lives we have the task of managing feelings and impulses that cannot be expressed in their original and undiluted form. We cannot just hit someone if we feel angry with them, we cannot just take a bar of chocolate from the shop if we want it, and we cannot have sex with any passing stranger just because we feel the urge. We do have to learn to modify our urges and manage the frustrations that come with growing up. We have to find ways of coping with just how painful that can be at times. The more painful our emotional experiences have been in the past the more pressure we are likely to feel to develop more extreme mechanisms of defence. The more we do that, the more we are likely to become detached from our own authentic selves. On the other hand, without defence mechanisms we would be too much exposed to insult injury and abuse, and the everyday hurts and minor mistreatments would be so keenly felt that we would not be able to carry on and function. In very extreme circumstances a person can become so detached from their own authentic self as to be deemed to have developed a serious mental illness. They no longer know who they are or how to use their own mind.

These defence mechanisms become established aspects of our personalities and we can be identified by the ways in which we try to protect ourselves from psychic pain. People are talked about in respect of their defence mechanisms, the person who is scared of enclosed spaces, or who cannot sustain relationships, or runs away from spiders, all these are everyday examples of fears and anxieties that come to form a part of the picture of that person's character.

We have seen in this chapter the role of defence mechanisms in our everyday lives, and how they can thought about in relation to a very simple, but useful model of the mind. We develop them to protect us from psychological pain. But actually they are called upon before the pain actually happens, we use them to prevent the pain being felt, not just to alleviate pain that has already happened. When we anticipate a painful situation developing we are alerted to this by feelings of anxiety and fear. It is these fears that trigger the defence mechanisms that we hope will enable to avoid the pain.

It is also anxiety that propels us to form defence mechanisms. We need to revisit the previous chapter here for a moment in order to elaborate this piece of the picture. Anxiety is a form of worry, or anticipation of something unpleasant, unwanted. At a simple, and useful level, it alerts us to the possibility that there is a problem to which we need to attend. If we feel anxious in the weeks before an exam this feeling may motivate us to revise in preparation for the exam. This would be a sensible way in which to both prepare for the exam and alleviate the anxiety. If we then feel less anxious because we are confident that we are well prepared, we are likely to perform as well as possible in the exam. However if we attempt to escape the anxiety by pretending that we do not care about the exam, or by going to the pub and getting drunk instead of working, or indeed by a process of denial that we even have an exam coming up, we will not ultimately tackle the anxiety, indeed we are likely to heighten it, precisely because we have not tackled the actual cause of anxiety.

One way of thinking about this is that if we repress or deny our original feelings and thoughts, we are likely to become anxious about how they may return. If we displace those original feelings on to something else, we will become anxious about the something else.

A woman that I once worked with had a terror of enclosed spaces, in particular elevators. As a child she had been locked in a small cupboard if she was disobedient. During her therapy we came to understand that it was not the enclosed space which terrified her, but her overwhelming feelings of rage and injustice that she was not allowed to express but had to keep locked inside herself. Her feelings were locked in a space that felt too small for them. As she got older she remained anxious that her rage would one day burst out of its cage and cause terrible harm to those that she loved. She displaced this anxiety onto small spaces like the elevator and felt overwhelmingly frightened at the thought of going into one. It took a long time for her to be able to think about her rage instead of thinking about elevators, but gradually as she began to find a little more courage to face her angry feelings she began to allow herself to know more about just how furious she actually felt. As she did so she became more able to contemplate using an elevator, though she never liked them and continued to avoid them if possible. What she did understand was that she was anxious about the feelings that she had repressed, and that she was anxious because she had repressed them and thus they always threatened to return.

Anxiety can be a very general state of mind. Some people are perpetually anxious and this is called generalised anxiety disorder.

They seem to feel anxious and to then look for something to be anxious about. If they do not have something to worry about they find something. They seem to carry with them a sense of something somewhere being wrong and they look around for what that might be. They usually find something since there are always some sort of problems and difficulties. Such people could be described as insecure and this may be to do with never having felt completely safe in their environment, or to do with having grown up with anxious parents. When we are with people who are anxious we tend to pick it up, it tends to be somewhat infectious and we sense it and feel it for ourselves.

This chapter has given a brief overview of the main terms to do with the development and purpose of defence mechanisms. These are measures that we unconsciously put in place in an attempt to protect ourselves from psychic pain. We need them to enable us to continue to function in our everyday lives, but they can come to control and limit our capacity to function well if they become too extreme.

The next chapter will discuss the way in which psychoanalysis considers that the thoughts and feelings which give rise to defence mechanisms can be addressed so as to fully resolve the problems to which they would otherwise lead.

FIVE

Remembering, repeating, and working through

"Those who cannot remember the past are condemned to repeat it" (1905).

George Santanya wrote this often quoted, and misquoted, sentence in a paper called "Reason in common sense".

In 1993, Maya Angelou wrote a poem for the inauguration of the American President, Bill Clinton, which included the lines: "History, despite its wrenching pain, cannot be unlived, but if faced with courage, need not be lived again."

In both cases the authors were thinking of social and political history, of wars and injustice. They were saying that if only we could learn from historical events, we could avoid making the same mistakes and build a better future for ourselves and our children. But what is implied in their comments is an awareness that we have a tendency to *not* learn the lessons of history, that we have a tendency to repeat the mistakes that have been made over and over again, to create war, misery, to deliberately generate human distress, to behave in brutal and inhuman ways toward our fellows, to be destructive rather than creative.

What is implied in Maya Angelou's lines is that we have some difficulty in facing the "wrenching pain" of history, of remembering it for long enough to properly face it, rather than live it again. On the other hand remembering, and remembrance, can, if done properly, lead to development, growth, to real change and a better world.

The comments quoted above, and many more that are so similar in sentiment, can be thought about, not just in the context of social and political life, but in the more immediate context of the individual human psyche, and that of families and groups. The question of whether an individual can remember, rather than choose to forget, their own past painful experiences, whether they can face up to the humiliations that they have suffered and that they have inflicted, whether they can face up to themselves, remember and work through their own internal difficulties, will have a huge impact on the extent to which they can ensure that the mistakes of the past are not repeated, but are understood as far as possible. In this way it is to be hoped that the future can be approached with an open mind and a conscious awareness of our own internal conflicts that may have an influence on the decisions that we make, and the way in which we relate to others.

Perhaps the first questions that need to be addressed are to do with the definitions of the terms. What is meant by the words "remembering" "repeating" and "working through" in this context of psychoanalytic thought? Since the study of psychoanalysis is the study of unconscious psychological processes, we could ask what is meant by the terms "unconscious remembering", "unconscious repeating", and "unconscious working through".

This then becomes a somewhat different discussion from what we usually associate with ordinary or conscious remembering and repeating.

Remembering can be thought of as the act of consciously recalling to mind an event from the past. If we meet someone for the second time we might remember meeting them previously.

We might remember their name, the circumstances in which we met them and the impression that they made upon us. We might remember the conversation that we had. This is where our memory might become a little less objective, we might remember something different from that which the other person remembers. Or we may remember the same conversation differently from that person. Much of what we think we remember is actually to do with perceptions and how we mentally reconstruct an event at a later point.

Two people, A and B met and had a conversation at a party. B later told the host of the party that the conversation had actually been a disagreement. A had not seen it that way at all and could not remember anything that was said that might have been construed as an argument. In fact A had no actual memory of the conversation at all and only knew that it happened because of what was later reported back to the host. A and B were active participants in the same conversation and yet their memory of it, or perception of it, was entirely different. Which one had the accurate memory would be impossible to establish. It is probable that B no longer remembers the conversation, but she does remember that for her it was an experience of conflict, of discomfort. If she ever has cause to think of A, she will link A's name with the feeling of being in a conflict, perhaps of feeling angry. It would be the feelings that would be recalled and remembered, and possibly re-experienced again, rather than the actual conversation.

My father died some years ago. There is much that I miss about him, about his presence that I remember in the missing of it. One of the things that I miss, is the sound of his voice. I do not miss the words that he used to say, but the deep sonorous tone of his voice. I suppose that when I was a little girl I found the tone of his voice very reassuring, it told me that he was nearby and that therefore I had his protection, his love and his interest in my well-being.

I do not remember consciously being aware of such thoughts or feelings, and I cannot recall much of what he actually said, but I know that my sense of loss now is linked to a desire to hear his voice again, and to a remembering of the sound of his voice.

What is also clear from these examples is that I am actually discussing forgetting as much as remembering, the one is indissolubly linked to the other, we cannot consider remembering without also and inextricably considering forgetting.

As always, Freud (1914g) had something to say about this. He wrote "Remembering, repeating and working through" in which he posed the questions, why do we remember some things and not others? Is this chance or is there more to it? Is there a reason for forgetting? What happens to the experiences that we have that we forget? Where do they go in our psyche? Why do we forget some experiences?

If we think back to the discussion on repression we can begin to link up some of the concepts that have been outlined so far, and consider how it is that experiences that have caused us psychic pain have been repressed, pushed away, forgotten. This would be especially true of painful experiences for which we have no language, no cognitive frame in which to formulate a comprehension of the experience. Children do not begin to use language as a means of comprehension until about the age of two years old, but they do have powerful experiences of sensations before that age. What sort of memory does that create? How does an infant know that it has a tummy ache if it does not have the words for tummy ache? What do we do with a memory sense of an event that we could not comprehend because we did not have the facility, the language, to comprehend it at the time?

Emotional experiences that are felt to be overwhelming, too full of conflict that cannot be processed, and with which no one seems to be able to help us, these are the experiences that may have to be repressed because they cannot be understood.

Sometimes repression is encouraged as a way of attempting to "get over" an emotional difficulty. The classic British "stiff upper lip" is an example. If you feel upset just push it all down, put a brave face on it and pretend it never happened.

But you can take this philosophy too far as we have discussed in the chapter on defence mechanisms.

Freud was interested in developing the techniques of the psychoanalytic treatment. He had tried and discarded hypnosis and thought that a more useful method was to get his patients to "free associate" that is, to say whatever came into their mind without restraint. He also began to listen carefully to their dreams. What he was beginning to understand was that whilst we may forget our past experiences, they do get expressed, and repeated, in our everyday lives and in our dreaming sleep. We may not realise that we are repeating that which we have forgotten, but it does seem that we are compelled to go over and over the same old ground in some way or another, unless and until we can face the past with courage, and move on from it, taking with us a full awareness of it, and a better awareness of our own internal psychological makeup.

A middle-aged man, Roger, was being treated for anxiety and depression. He was having panic attacks and pacing the floor in the middle of the night desperately trying to find a way of stopping thoughts in his head that were indeed quite mad, that he should commit suicide, or cut himself, or hurt someone else. He came from a family in which any kind of emotional crisis was managed by trying not to think about it. If something was upsetting then just don't think about it, think about something else, forget it. This principle was applied to all emotional situations big and small, so if someone important had died, or if he had just stubbed his toe, the same approach was used, don't think about it.

As a result Roger did not learn to think about his feelings at all and did not learn to differentiate between a big emotional crisis and a small emotional dilemma. They were all big to him and he had no way of dealing with them. When he became a teenager he took drugs, which took the dilemmas away temporarily, but he took too many and eventually caused himself serious injury when he was involved in an accident whilst he was high on drink and drugs. As he lay in his hospital bed with his arms and legs in plaster, he knew that he had to make some serious changes but he had no resources within himself to think about this beyond a rather futile resolution to never take drugs again. He needed a lot of help to begin to learn to think about his feelings rather than just push them away. He needed a lot of support to tolerate the pain of having to think, of having to face the "wrenching pain" of his own emotional history.

Roger had not grown up in a bad family, his parents were loving and kind and he had a sibling with whom he had a warm relationship. He was not actively mistreated, but his need to learn to process his emotional experiences was not recognised. He had been taught to forget or repress, rather than to remember and work through. When he was a small child it was his parents who could not bear to remember and work through, it was they who could not handle very much emotional conflict, but as he grew up he was also unable to do this because he had not been helped to develop a capacity to face his own distressing feelings. When he moved into adolescence he sought out situations in which he both forgot his pain, but were also destructive. This drug induced obliteration of feelings meant that he did not work properly, did not care for his family properly, and could be thought of as a repeating, not of the emotional pain but of the anger and rage that he felt towards his parents for not helping him when he needed it. He was not aware of these feelings but his adult destructiveness suggested that he was reliving, re-enacting, and repeating unresolved feelings and emotional dilemmas from the past, of which he had no awareness.

Not only did his behaviour put him into real danger, it was his own behaviour that resulted in the very serious accident that he had, but he was also entering a world of unreality, he was living in a stupefied state of mind in which he did not have to deal with reality of everyday life, a fantasy world. His wife left him, he lost his job, he had no money, he was utterly miserable. The circle had turned, his emotional life had become overwhelmingly difficult and had ultimately caught up with him. And all because he did not know how to face up to himself. He did not know how to remember and work through, so he was compelled to repeat.

He repeated not only the emotional dilemmas that had not been addressed in his childhood, but also the defence mechanisms that he had been taught to use instead, and the anger and rage that he had felt about not being able to effectively work through his dilemmas. It is not just the actual situation that we repeat, and remember by repeating, but also the attendant emotional experiences of being dependent upon people who let us down in some way, and the seemingly inexpressible feelings towards those people, of which we are barely aware but which get expressed in the ways in which we deal with our adult selves and adult relationships.

Roger did this. He would get into a disagreement with someone and would not know how to manage this. He would take drugs in order to forget, to escape the confusion that he felt. In this way he repeated the original experience of being in conflict, and the defence mechanism that was employed. But he also caused his parents great pain by his behaviour and in this way he forced them to know about his pain and simultaneously punished them for doing so. He expressed his anger and rage with them.

People who are abused in some way as children, are vulnerable to this kind of repeating. Many of us will know someone like this in our own personal lives, someone who goes from one abusive relationship to another, just as bad. Someone who repeatedly engages in the same type of destructive behaviour. I know women who are obese, who perpetually attempt to diet, to follow a healthy eating regime, only to give up and return to their old eating habits, habits that they know will lead to weight gain and all the physical pain, restrictions, and health complications that this involves. Why do they do this? Why do they repeat self-destructive patterns that ultimately lead to a great deal of pain?

Well one reason might be that the eating, rather like Roger's drugs, somehow allows them to forget some sort of emotional pain for a time. Maybe this is why it is called comfort eating. It is not a real comfort, it is, like drugs, a pseudo comfort, that allows a temporary forgetting of emotional pain that cannot be faced because it is felt to be too overwhelming. The pain is repressed, but pain is also created, because with obesity comes a range of very painful health issues. What it also brings is a restricted life. People who are obese cannot be as active as others, and this also reflects the emotional situation in which the internal emotional life of the person is restricted by not being able to face themselves fully, by having to keep some aspects of self in chains, by not being free to be oneself to the full, to use the psychological self with a sense of freedom, unconstrained by fears of powerful feelings that are too much to bear.

Some of what cannot be remembered will be to do with emotional events before speech, too early to be consciously remembered or thought about.

But what Freud is suggesting, and what psychoanalysis had taken up and developed ever since, is that there is an alternative to a life sentence of repeating, and that is to remember and to work through. In therapy he suggested that just listening carefully to what people say, and to their dreams we can piece together a picture of how the repeating is taking place, how the past is being relived in the present, and of how this may in fact be a communication, a plea for help to remember and not just a way of escaping the past and forgetting.

When children are very young they know very little about the context in which they experience their lives. When a baby is hungry, it is unlikely to know that it is hungry, it is likely that it simply knows that it does not feel ok. It will not therefore be able to remember that it was hungry as a baby. It may however remember that having something put into its mouth to suck upon, resulted in feeling better. This would not be a conscious memory, but having felt hungry, or bad and then found a way to feel better (i.e, having discovered that the nipple or teat leads to a more comfortable feeling), the baby is likely to quickly connect the bad feeling with the need for a teat in its mouth. For cigarette smokers the feeling is the same, a sensation of discomfort leads to a wish or a need for a cigarette. The early means of comfort and relief of a sense of discomfort is repeated symbolically by the use of a cigarette. But it is often not felt as a choice, it is felt to be a need. Even though nobody actually needs to smoke a cigarette, it can quickly come to be experienced as a compulsive need. The "compulsion to repeat" is in place.

The compulsion to repeat is the next piece of the psychoanalytic conceptual jigsaw puzzle.

This term was used in the same paper, "Remembering, repeating and working through". Freud (1914g) He was discussing the process of psychoanalytic treatment, and in this context he says *we must be prepared to find therefore that the patient yields to the compulsion to repeat, which now replaces the impulsion to remember, not only in his attitude to the doctor but also in every other activity and relationship which may occupy his life at the time.* Freud goes on to assert that the stronger the repression, the more likely that the repeating will be compulsively enacted in a symbolic form. In other words the more deeply we attempt to bury our emotional life, the more we will be compelled to find ways of giving it expression, but we will do this without any conscious awareness that we are in fact repeating an old situation.

All the defence mechanisms that were discussed in chapter four involve the remembering and repeating that we are now discussing in Chapter Five.

This would be a bleak outlook if it were not for the notion that some good can come of these psychological processes, that there is an alternative to a life spent in the grip of repetition compulsion. I think it is reasonable to suppose that we do all know the strength of such a grip to different degrees since this is all part of the development of our individual personalities, but we need to believe that it is possible to move on from such powerful emotional chains and to think about how this is possible.

If we face the past and remember it instead of repeating it, how does this make a difference? What happens next? What does "working through" mean? How does it work and how does it make a difference? What is the purpose of working something through?

It is quite difficult to find a clear answer to this question. It is sometimes described as talking about something and going over it again and again until it no longer matters very much. This can be what it looks like from the outside, but in itself this is not working through, this is just talking until there is nothing left to say. We can spend as much time as we like talking over a problem and identifying the difficulty, but in itself this only achieves a clearer identification of the difficulty. This is necessary as a starting point but it is not the work of working through.

Working through was originally discussed in terms of the therapy relationship in which the patient talks about their past and the therapist listens and in particular attends to the way in which the past may be repeated in some way within the context of the therapy relationship. For example Roger, the young man mentioned above, found it very difficult to settle into therapy because even though the therapist was there to listen carefully and to think about his difficulties, he could not believe that she really was listening and would often say things like: "Oh but you don't want to hear all this". He was assuming that what could not be talked about in the past could not be talked about in this relationship either. The therapist could then notice this and talk to him about how his early experiences were influencing his way of relating to her. Because he was interested in himself he began to develop a capacity to think about this and to modify his perception of the therapist and also of others.

But this was a therapy situation. How does working through happen in other relationships that are not necessarily organised for the purpose of thinking carefully about someone's emotional difficulties.

The first criteria for working through is the presence of a relationship. In terms of this concept it is not possible for working through to take place outside of a relationship. Working through is to do with growth, and development, and this involves an acceptance of limitations as well as a discovery of potential. This has to take place in the context of a relationship with an other, with a mind that is not the same as one's own mind, that sees things a little differently, that has a different perspective, that has thoughts that are other than and different from one's own. A parent is an example of such an other as this. When a baby is crying because she is in discomfort, the parent or carer will say something like: "You are hungry", or "You are tired". In this way the infant gradually begins to differentiate one experience of discomfort from another, they learn that one feeling is hunger and another feeling is tiredness. But they also learn something far more profoundly important than this, and that is that it is possible to discover more of oneself through the close and caring relationship with an other. They do not know that this is what they are learning but it is so. Of course they may instead learn that discovering oneself is actually prohibited in the context of a relationship, as Roger had learned. But even Roger had somehow learned that he needed a relationship in order to get better so it is reasonable to suppose that somewhere along the line someone had offered him a sense of understanding that he had been able to take in and hold onto. Maybe it was a teacher or a nursery worker, but Roger was not devoid of the capacity to be in a relationship altogether, and he had had parents who did care for him even though they had their own emotional stumbling blocks.

What I am saying here is that we all need to be in relationship to others to grow emotionally, and we need a relationship to work through our difficulties with remembering so as not to repeat, or at least to repeat less.

What I am also saying here is that it is the fact that the relationship is with someone who has a mind of their own, that working through is possible.

The next criteria is that this someone does need to be interested in the mind of the person who is trying to work through. Interested and willing to engage in an attempt to understand and to offer their own thoughts about the problem that is to be worked through. It is reasonable to suppose that therapists are interested in their patients and how their minds work. It is also reasonable to suppose that friends, family, and maybe even colleagues are interested in the feelings of those around them.

A third criteria would be that the person with the problem needs to be interested in their own mind, they need to have a degree of curiosity about why they are the way they are and a willingness to face the past and to remember. Not everyone is curious about themselves and how they function psychologically.

Originally Roger did not want to work through his difficulties, he would have preferred to have had someone else just sort it all out for him so that he did not have to do the work himself. It took a long time and a lot of patient listening, before he very gradually began to find the courage to face the hurt and humiliation of the past. All the listening was supportive and helped him to accept the therapist as someone who was interested and did care about him, but it was all in preparation for the working through rather than being the work itself. It was not until Roger trusted both the therapist and himself enough to become more bold, more curious, that the working through could begin to happen.

For many people medication, distraction, and the use of defence mechanisms is preferable to working through, they are not willing to face the past, it is felt to be too painful too difficult and too pointless. Without this basic willingness, working through is stopped before it begins.

So far this discussion has identified the purpose of working through, which is to grow and develop emotionally, and two criteria needed for the task, a relationship with an interested other, and a curiosity about oneself. But it still remains to attempt to understand what it is, what happens.

What happened with Roger in therapy, and what can happen in the context of other relationships that meet the above criteria, is that gradually Roger began to psychologically shake loose the chains of his past. The more he remembered it the less frightening it seemed. As he was able to talk about one remembered event it came to seem more possible to remember another, and the likelihood that the remembering might not be as devastating as he had expected, grew. As the therapist seemed to be able to face and accept his feelings, so he became more able to face them. This again is not unlike the ideal situation for a baby who is in distress. If the mother or carer can cope with the baby's distress with empathy, then the baby can come to understand that distress is not the end of the world, and that it can be tolerated and some relief can be found. If however the mother is highly anxious and panics when the baby is in distress, then the baby does not have an experience of being in an environment in which the distress is tolerable and a solution can be thoughtfully found. Their own feelings can become more, rather than less frightening.

We all have the same situations as adults. If we are upset we seek someone who will help us to remember that this is not the end of the world, that we can bear it and we will find a way to cope with it. Even as adults we cannot always do this for ourselves, we need another caring, loving person to help us with it.

Turning to another is the first stage of working through.

Learning to allow that person to help us to bear our distress is the second stage.

What this achieves is the creation of some mental space, some room in our minds to stay with the feelings that we have, but also to think about them. This is the essence of working through. Working through is not to do with getting rid of feelings or necessarily of changing them, but it is to do with having them and thinking about them. Much of the work at this point may take place just within our own minds, but it has the context of a caring relationship.

If we can think about our own feelings with a degree of curiosity, we can possibly think about other people's feelings with curiosity. So Roger for example gradually began to notice his own feelings and to wonder if what he felt was what he really felt or if it was a way of pushing aside his real feelings. He then began to ask why it was that his parents always told him to just forget any event that caused him distress. He felt very angry with them for a time, that they had not had the strength to cope with his childlike distress, but he also began to realise that they had issues of their own which made emotional distress seem unbearable to them. In this way he gradually began to clear his head, to sort through the miasma of confused feelings and to understand and accept reality.

He did this in the context of a relationship in which he had access to the interest and concern of an other, in this instance the therapist.

Working through is a step by step process which takes place in the context of a caring relationship, and in which the person gradually becomes able and brave enough to think about their past and to think about the way in which they use their own mind. It is a process of tolerating painful feelings and at the same time taking enough of a step back from them to think about them. In this way a greater capacity to use one's own mind freely, is developed.

It does not need to be therapy that facilitates this working through. When we first fall in love as teenagers or young adults, we often undertake a whole reassessment of ourselves as a result of our discovery of our love for another. It is also not unusual for young people, to find themselves working through their own relationship with their parents in the light of becoming parents themselves. They may do this together as a couple in the interests of bringing up their children in the best way that they can.

If we can do this, is we can remember the "wrenching pain" rather than repeat, or live it again, we can begin to work through, with the help of others, and working through can lead to the freedom to use our minds and our experiences in more thoughtful ways.

But perhaps the most common experience that has to be worked through for everyone, is that of loss. We all suffer losses of all sorts throughout life and each time this happens we have to face the feelings, accept the loss and think about the future. We also all suffer trauma. For some people this is huge trauma and for others it is more everyday shocks. Trauma includes a considerable degree of thinking about loss, and about how loss involves the processes of remembering, repeating and working through.

SIX

Envy and guilt

It may seem curious at first glance that of all the human emotions and feelings that might be well placed in an introduction to psychoanalytic thinking, envy and guilt find their way in. What about happiness, or sorrow, love or hate, pain or joy? Are they not more obvious emotional conditions to include here?

Melanie Klein (1921–1945) wrote about envy and guilt in her seminal book, *Love, Guilt and Reparation*. In this book she put envy and guilt firmly on the psychoanalytic map as central emotional experiences with which we all have to grapple and which have to be negotiated and renegotiated in many everyday encounters and relationships. We are inclined to compare ourselves with everyone we meet, all the time. We wonder if the person sitting next to us is prettier, wealthier, and cleverer. We might have a better car than one person, but it is not so good as another's. We might live in a bigger house than the family over the road, but a smaller house than the wealthy people a few miles away. We constantly, consciously and unconsciously rank ourselves in relation to those around us. If the way in which we rank ourselves in relation to another person is roughly in line with the way in which they rank themselves in relation to us, then we are more or less in tune with each other, but if we are out of tune with each other, the relationship will be constantly battling with misunderstanding and indeed competition. For example in a workplace setting there may be two people who have to work together who both consider themselves to be senior to the other. It is not difficult to imagine how this may give rise to friction between them. The degree of friction may in some respects reflect a measure of the difficulty of resolving feelings of envy.

In order to think about envy we need to distinguish it from jealousy. This chapter will outline a distinction between the two for the purposes of this discussion, though the two concepts have become more or less synonymous in everyday usage. For the most part we are interested in the place of envy in everyday life and also the importance of guilt and reparation.

In ordinary everyday conversation, the words jealousy and envy are frequently used interchangeably and can mean much the same thing. In psychoanalysis, and historically, they have distinctly separate meanings.

Jealousy is used to denote the feeling of wanting what someone else has got.

It can include admiration, aspiration, and can inspire a determination to do well, to work hard, to achieve. When we are jealous of someone we see something that we think we would like to have. We may accept that it will never be for us, but we might go on from this position to work towards having something that we can have, that is inspired by the jealousy that we feel about what someone else has.

Someone else has something that we admire and wish for, and we too can have something that is admirable and be in a position of feeling pleased with our own achievements.

Jealousy can also be to do with the anxiety that something that one values will be taken away, especially a relationship. We talk of jealous lovers, or of guarding jealously. This form of jealousy recognises the value and importance of a person, or perhaps a possession, but in valuing it, feels terribly worried that someone else will want to take it away, or to spoil. It is as though the jealousy recognises the next step to an envious attack on the security of the very thing that is so precious.

For example Roy, at the age of eighteen years old left school with a couple of A-levels and started work in a small firm that was developing a new form of technology to help people with sight impairment to use computers more easily. The managing director of this small firm was a very enthusiastic, dedicated man, who was convinced that his ideas were workable, necessary, and useful. Roy felt jealous of his boss's confidence. Roy was uncertain of himself and uncertain that he had the natural abilities to make a significant contribution to the team. He looked at his boss and wished he could be more like the boss. He also wished that he could be the boss. Roy was able to appreciate that he was young and just starting out and he resolved to try to achieve success in order to feel more self-confident. He also resolved to work hard enough and become authoritative enough to become a boss in a workplace setting one day. Roy used his jealousy of his boss, his wish to have something of what he saw in his boss, to inform his own approach to his career, he learned from his jealousy, something of his own wishes, and he used this awareness to make a decision about how he would try to have something for himself that was rather like what he admired in his boss. His boss, in turn, rather enjoyed the experience of being held in high esteem by Roy. He felt appreciated and that Roy's admiration for him reflected all the hard work he had put into attaining the position he now had. He was secure enough in his own value to not feel threatened by Roy but to wish Roy well and to want to help him to develop his skills and become successful as well. This was a mutually appreciative and rewarding relationship in which a successful man helped a younger man to become successful, and in which the motivating feeling was one of jealousy, of "I want what that person is able to have". The feeling of jealousy, the feeling of lacking something that is desired, diminished as the relationship between the two men developed and became more mutually satisfying. Gradually they realised that whilst they were different from one another, they both offered the other an opportunity to experience a sense of well-being and that the relationship that they had was of value to both of them in different ways.

A very different scenario was unfolding for Roy in connection with another colleague who was on the same level as him. Both young men were also enthusiastic football supporters.

Phillip was an ambitious person but he carried within himself an underlying fear of failure. He was a member of a family in which there was an assumption that all the children would do well. His older brother and sisters had achieved high academic and professional status and it was assumed that Phillip would do the same. This was experienced as a considerable pressure by Phillip who dreamed of being successful, in order to be in a position to stop trying to be successful. But of course whenever he did achieve something the next goal was just waiting in line, and as the youngest in the family he had always felt that he could never catch up with his siblings. At an unconscious level Phillip was furious about this. His anger and rage was usually displaced onto something else, and he played football with considerable aggression and determination to win. Equally he watched football matches with a passion and if his team did not win he found it difficult to contain his rage. Sometimes he did get into fights with other football supporters though he was clever enough to avoid being caught or arrested.

In the workplace Roy and Phillip formed a fairly natural alliance in that they were both young, both football fans and both ambitious and wanting to advance their careers in as rewarding a way as possible.

However whilst Roy's approach was to listen and learn and to value what their boss could teach them, Phillip resented his boss's greater knowledge and senior position. Roy valued and wanted to guard his sense of his own potential to achieve his ambitions, he did not want to risk losing this by becoming vengeful and bitter. Phillip on the other hand would try to find fault with the decisions that were made, and would make fun of the boss behind his back. His conversation would imply that he thought that he himself would make a better job of being the boss. Like Roy he could see that the boss had something of value, something that he wanted, but unlike Roy, Phillip harboured an underlying hatred of the person who seemed to have what he wanted and felt that he lacked. He wanted to get rid of this feeling of lack, of inadequacy and this became focused on wishing that he could get rid of the boss.

Roy was jealous and protective of his own sense of ambition, but he did not feel destructive towards his boss, but Phillip was envious, because he wanted to get rid of the person who was the focus of his angry feelings, the person who made him feel a sense of lack in himself.

In psychoanalytic terms jealousy is to do with wanting what someone else has, like success, but not wanting to take it from them, simply wanting that for oneself.

Envy is wanting what someone else has in a destructive way, wanting to take it from that other person, to prevent them from having it.

Envy can go further than this, it can go as far as wanting to destroy the very thing that one desires, rather than let someone else continue to have it. Had Phillip's attempts to sabotage the reputation of his boss, been too successful, he would have brought the company into disrepute and they would have lost customers and investors. This could have led to the failure of the company, the very thing that Phillip needed to pay his salary, and wanted to be in charge of himself one day.

Many examples of envious rage and its consequences can be found in fairy tales.

Rapunzel, Sleeping Beauty, Cinderella, all have characters consumed with envy, and it is this envy that causes all the problems in the story and threatens to destroy all the goodness.

In Snow White for example, the wicked step mother is unable to cope with the fact she is getting older and losing her youthful good looks, and Snow White is changing from a girl into a lovely young woman. She tries to destroy Snow White in the false hope that this will mean that she herself will retain her beauty, but the more evil deeds she commits the more ugly she becomes. She cannot see that it is envy that is destroying all the beauty, including her own. She sets out to destroy the very thing that she desires, which is beauty, rather than accept that it belongs to someone else now.

One of the ideas for which Sigmund Freud (1908c) is famous, is his concept of penis envy. He maintained that girls become aware of their own lack at an early age, when they realise that boys have something that they do not have. The partner theory to penis envy is castration anxiety, the fear experienced by boys that the part of their body that is so representative of masculinity and potency, will be attacked and destroyed. Freud considered that at the age of around three to four years old the small boy enters into a stage of development in which he seeks to compete with his father for the love of his mother. He fears that the father will punish him through castration for this attempt to achieve masculine primacy. This is a process which can be noticed in a more simplistic way in the animal world where the young males oust the older males in order to become the head of the herd.

Melanie Klein (1937 [1921–1945]) had another idea about envy which did not directly contradict Freud but did challenge and develop his notion of penis envy. She maintained that the major focus of our envy is the maternal body. She thought that when we are very young babies, much earlier than three or four years old, we unconsciously experience great conflict in our feelings towards the body that gave us life. To begin with we imagine that we simply own the mother, she is not a separate being but an extension of our own bodily self that we conjure up when we are hungry or we want to play or we need a cuddle. Gradually we have to learn that actually our mother is not part of us, or even something we can control but a separate person, mind, and body. We are curious, fascinated and hugely indebted to her and to her body. But we are also very angry about the fact that she does not belong to us, and that we have to relinquish ownership of her. Klein suggested that we have unconscious phantasies to do with the internal world of the maternal body, that it is full of other things, other babies, or penises, or faeces, and that we want to get back inside it, get rid of these other contents and resume ownership of the maternal space. In developing these ideas, which can sound very farfetched, she is putting envy and destructive rage at the heart of what it is to be human.

A young boy of about four or five years old, was met from school by the baby sitter. He had been expecting his mother to meet him but she had needed to do something else at that time. He was not happy about seeing the baby sitter at the school gates but he did not protest too much until they got home when he began to be rude and to refuse to do what was being asked of him. He said that he wanted some sweets and was told that he could not have any until his behaviour improved. He then punched the baby sitter in the stomach. She was shocked by the depth of rage that was behind the blow and the fact that he deliberately aimed for her stomach. She felt that he should have known that hitting a woman in the stomach was particularly unacceptable.

I wondered if he was actually furious with his mother for not being available to him when he wanted and expected her to be. In his anger he felt as though he was like a helpless baby who had no power to change the situation. It may be that he displaced his rage with his mother onto the baby sitter, but more than this, he attacked the specific area of the body that represented the maternal space, where once he had sole occupation, before birth, but now he had been ejected from that space and could never reign supreme there again. It seems to me and it seemed to the baby sitter that he had deliberately aimed for that particular part of her body, that he particularly hated and wanted to hurt, that part of her at that moment, which is so symbolic of her maternal capacity. He hated it because he could not have it, so he attacked it in an envious attempt to destroy that which he longed for but could not possess.

When there are media stories of girls or young women who are raped, sometimes viciously raped, I am reminded of Melanie Klein's theories. It seems as though the young men who commit these acts cannot bear the fact that the woman's body and its interior space belongs to her and not to them and they would prefer to destroy it altogether than to come to terms with the fact that they cannot own it. Instead they invade that interior space in order to hurt, damage and sometimes destroy it.

Indeed if one looks at many societies throughout history, there is an ongoing story of the different ways in which men, women and social groups, have been unable to tolerate the notion of women's independence or control over their own minds and bodies. Melanie Klein, and subsequent psychoanalytic thinkers would suggest that this is to do with the envy and rage towards the maternal body and the difficulty of the task for some people, both male and female, of relinquishing an unconscious phantasy of having control and ownership of it.

The important difference between envy and jealousy is that envy leads to destruction, to emptiness, whereas jealousy is not destructive and can lead to development if it can be acknowledged for what it is.

But what is to be done about envious, destructive rage? If as very small infants we feel, albeit unconsciously, such furious rage towards our mother where does that leave us, or take us in our further development?

Melanie Klein, and the school of psychoanalysis since she was writing, would argue that we all feel this furious rage as small infants, but that if we are lucky enough to have a mother or carer who can tolerate and accept our rage, who can intuitively understand that it is difficult to have to learn that we are not the boss, and who can gently teach us that we will be all right if we accept that we do not have sole ownership of her, then this loving understanding combined with a firm encouragement towards accepting our own smallness, can enable us to grow as a person. It can enable us to appreciate that with development comes loss, the loss of the phantasy that we are in control in this instance, but that without development we cannot grow into fully functioning human beings.

When we, as a small infant can feel the rage, but also feel the loving response, then we are likely to be able to begin to feel a wish to return the love that is given to us, to feel concern for the maternal object, and this in turn can lead to an understanding that we have something of value to offer our mother/carer as well as having needs to be met. This is the beginning of the capacity to feel guilt, which in turn leads to the wish to make reparation.

Someone was talking to me recently about their own early experience of writing a book. Her book was a very ambitious project that required a lot of research and took a long time to produce. She had been encouraged in this endeavour by the publisher who had originally suggested to her that she was the right person to write the book and that it was something she would do well. She was, of course, flattered by this and decided to take on the project. At this point she could be thought of as feeling like the baby who is basking in the warmth and admiration of an adoring mother, those early feelings might have been evoked again. The encouragement sustained her sense of worth as she researched and wrote the book, and she felt that she and the publisher were in tune with each other, that there was no conflict between them. She finished the first draft and sent it to the publisher who promptly sent it to another colleague to review and critique it. This was felt by the writer to be a sort of betrayal. Even though she knew that this was standard practice, she had been buoyed up during the months of writing by the hopeful wish that the publisher would receive the news of its completion with unmitigated joy and would immediately set about presenting the book to the world as the latest masterpiece in the field. Her fantasy was that the book would be received in the way that the birth of a new baby is received, as little short of a miracle.

After some months the draft was returned to her from the reviewer and it was covered in comments, criticisms and suggestions. The author felt outraged, she felt that she had been tricked into thinking that she was able to produce this work successfully, that she had been knowingly seduced into doing a great deal of research that was now being sadistically trashed, and she felt utterly humiliated. At that point she hated the publisher and the reviewer, and wanted nothing to do with him.

We can link this part of the story to the foregoing discussion to do with envy. At this point, the publisher stands in for a parental figure who is perceived to have the power to make the person feel wonderful or to make them feel ridiculous. The young man, Phillip in the previous example, felt like this about his parents and older siblings, that their praise could make him feel good about himself, but their ridicule could also make him feel contemptible. Whilst a person in this position feels good they do not have to be aware of the fact that this feeling is dependent on the other person, but as soon as they feel humiliated they are put in touch with just how fragile and dependent they really are, and how it is the other person who has the power and not them. This would be at the root of their envious attitude to that person, their wish to destroy that which feels as though it has the power to destroy them.

In the author's case she symbolically destroyed the publisher, by deleting the returned draft containing the reviewers comments and sending a bitter email protesting that she worked hard for a long time for nothing and would not be writing anything for that particular publisher ever again.

Fortunately the publisher was good at understanding just how humiliating it can feel to have a piece of work returned in that way, and she decided to retain a copy of the critiqued draft and to wait for a while. In this respect she responded rather like a parent who decides to just wait until the infant has calmed down and then to try to generate a more measured response to the criticism, in a way, to turn envious destructive rage into a more constructive even if jealous, way forward.

In a fairly short space of time the author began to regret her hasty and angry actions and also felt rather guilty about some of the thoughts that she had had towards the publisher, which had been less than kind. She began to realise that the author had given her an opportunity and encouragement and that this was still available to her. It was her fantasies about what the encouragement had meant that had been out of step with the reality. She had chosen to believe that the encouragement meant that she was someone special, perfect. She *was* someone special but the task that she had undertaken was a big challenge and one with which she was bound to need help and advice and this had to involve criticism. She began to realise that the criticism sprang from a wish to help her, not to humiliate her and that it was her own grandiose fantasies that led to her sense of shame and ridicule, not the criticism.

When she had worked through these angry and then guilty feelings she wanted to make reparation and she wanted her book to survive her own envious attack and be published. She made an approach to the publisher under the guise of a completely different matter, but used the opportunity to ask the publisher if she had a copy of the critiqued manuscript because she had mislaid her own.

The publisher rightly heard this communication as an apology and a dialogue was opened up between them. The book was given further attention, further work was put into it and sometime later it was published. It was a great success and this was duly attributed to the author, the publisher, and the reviewer.

The book can be thought of as a kind of baby. Its conception was exciting, its gestation was a long period of continued work as it gradually developed. As with the birth of a baby, the mother could not do this alone, she needed the help of a midwife/reviewer to bring the baby/book out into the world. At the culmination of all this there could be a celebration, a rejoicing, but the process of gestation involved working through hatred, rage, envy, destructiveness, through to acceptance, gratitude, and respect for the other. And importantly respect for one's own need of the other, respect for one's own limitations as well as one's own creativity.

It can be seen from this discussion that the unpleasant feelings of jealousy can be used to promote a desire and a drive to work hard and to become more successful in one's own right.

On the other hand jealousy can turn sour and become envy. But in turn envy can, with help, become something more productive.

The early Christian Church identified what have become known as the seven deadly sins. They are called deadly for good reason. They are; wrath, greed, sloth, pride, lust, envy, and gluttony. The list conjures up a picture of lazy thoughtless desire to have everything for nothing. But of all of them envy is considered the worst because envy is at the root of a destructive attack on what is desired at the expense of anything worthwhile. If it cannot be modified it leaves a barren landscape in its wake.

Another rather different example is of two young men were walking home late one night. They had long hair, wore shorts and t shirts, and were laughing and talking together about music. They were jumped on by a group of seven other young men, who had short hair, wore jeans and hooded sweaters. They were not chatting but looking for excitement. The seven men set about beating up the two and were only interrupted by the arrival of a couple of older men who disturbed them.

It was a senseless attack on two people who were minding their own business, and could not lead to any kind of positive outcome.

As they were never caught it is not possible to know why the seven behaved in the way that they did, but it is possible to suggest that they were acting from an unconscious envy. They could not tolerate that the two men wore different clothes from their own uniform, or that they were absorbed in their own conversation, from which the group of seven were excluded. They wanted the two men to feel the sense of isolation and vulnerability that they themselves felt and found unbearable, but could not acknowledge. Their envy of the contented state of mind of the two men stirred up such hatred in them that they set about destroying it, with no purpose other than destruction and intimidation. This is a relatively mild example of how envious hatred can lead to senseless pain. There are many examples in the course of an ordinary day, of the many and varied ways in which envy causes misery to no good effect either for the victim or for the perpetrator and this is why it is considered to be the deadliest of the deadly sins.

If envy takes a hold of a person, it can dominate their relationships with others, but also with themselves. It is possible that if a person's way of being is too full of hatred, then any thoughts or ideas that they may have that are more generous or more in search of warmth and affection, will have to be denied a space in their mind. Sometimes one comes across people who are consumed by bitterness and very unhappy, but who cannot bear to allow that they are inflicting this unhappiness upon themselves by refusing to begin to think that the problem might be their own rather than belonging to someone else. In this way they attack their own capacity to create a loving space in their mind in which something more productive can grow, because they cannot bear the humiliating task of acknowledging that they feel a sense of lack. They feel inadequate in the face of their own needs, so they choose to deny their own needy feelings rather than have to feel them. When they do have a more creative thought or idea it is pushed aside by an aspect of their own mind that tells them that such a thought does not belong to the dominant order and cannot be permitted. The loss that this involves is also denied and the sense of emptiness that follows is experienced as another reason to feel hate and rage rather than an awareness of one's own self-defeating emotional processes. Phillip was rather like this. He could not bear his own sense of feeling small and longing for admiration. Whenever such feelings threatened to emerge into his conscious awareness, he pushed them away by furiously turning to thoughts of angry destruction and hate. Thus the very part of his mind that might have been able to help him with his own destructiveness was attacked and treated as though it was a denigrated and worthless piece of rubbish. This would never help Phillip to find any sense of real achievement. Were he to continue in this way he would never discover his own strengths, precisely because he could not face his own limitations.

This chapter has looked at the meanings of the words jealousy and envy, and at the process of moving from envy to guilt and reparation. Jealousy can often be acknowledged and is not destructive, envy is rarely felt as such, it is felt as rage and hatred and is nihilistic in its aim. Everyone has to deal with their own feelings that are generated by a perception of being in some way lacking in relation to another person, and indeed with the feeling that someone else is envious or jealous of oneself. It is an underlying feature of many daily interactions at all sorts of levels of relationship. It can even be a feature of our relationship with our self.

The following three chapters are to do with the concepts of transference, counter transference, and projective identification, and these concepts help us to think about the unconscious processes by which feelings such as jealousy and envy, can be communicated between people in spoken and unspoken ways. They help us to consider how we can know something more of our own internal world and to some extent that of the other people with whom we come into contact in our everyday lives.

SEVEN

Transference

The concept of transference is at the heart of psychoanalytic understanding about the relationship between a clinician and a patient. It is not only at the heart of understanding but is the central focus of a psychoanalytic treatment. This means that a psychoanalytically trained clinician will always be thinking about what is going on in the transference aspect of the therapy relationship, and will base their comments to the patient upon this understanding. This process is known as "formulating an interpretation".

Transference is central to a psychoanalytic treatment between an individual patient and a psychotherapist and it is in the context of such a treatment that the concept has been developed and discussed and argued over. But it is also a concept that can be useful in understanding aspects of relationships other than the treatment relationship. It is a concept that can help to understand that between a teacher and a student, or between a doctor or nurse and a patient, or between a carer and a cared for person. What all these relationships have in common is that one person needs something from the other person, that they have a degree of dependency upon the other person, and it is this dependency that can give rise to the phenomena that we call transference. The dependency can be great as in the situation of a very ill person who needs the medical staff to make them well again, or it can be small, as in needing help to spell an unfamiliar word.

Whatever the situation, when we need or even just require something from another person, we can be said to be in a transference relationship to them.

If we can understand what this idea called transference is all about, we can use it to help us to manage our own feelings and understand the behaviour of others, better than might have been possible before.

In order to understand what transference is, it is necessary to have an overview of the story of how the concept was first developed and the way in which it is has evolved and grown in the years since Sigmund Freud first used the term. We can think about how it can be accurately and usefully applied in other situations. We can also think about those aspects of communication with another person that do not involve transference.

Freud (1912b) wrote "The dynamics of transference" and in this paper he said:

> If someone's need for love is not entirely satisfied by reality, he is bound to approach every new person whom he meets with libidinal anticipatory ideas; and it is highly probable that both portions of his libido, the portion that is capable of becoming conscious as well as the unconscious one, have a share in forming that attitude. (p. 100)

What is he saying here, what does this mean?

I think that when Freud uses the term "love" he does not just mean the devoted love of a parent for a child or the intensity of love between lovers, or within families. I think he is using the word love to include care, affection, and friendship. I think he means the whole spectrum of loving feelings that are possible for people to have and to share with each other.

Equally when he says "someone's need for love" I think he does not just mean their need to be loved but also their need to give love. I believe that the need to be allowed to offer our love to others is equally as important to us as the need to feel loved by others. This is apparent in our need to help others and to play our part in the society and community in which we live. If we choose to take up an occupation that involves helping other people, we are wanting to find ways in which we can offer our lovingness to that community of people, to our colleagues, to other members of the organisation, and to the people who are served by the task of the organisation. We want our offerings to be accepted and valued. We do not just want to be loved in return but to be allowed to know that we have within us the means to be of value to others.

This is a need that does not necessarily feel like a need, but it is so nevertheless.

But Freud is saying that when the need to love and be loved is not or has not, been satisfied by reality, in other words, when we do not feel very much loved or cared for, and do not feel that anyone wants our love or care, he is saying that we will approach everyone we meet with this particular unfulfilled need. We will also approach everyone we meet with a desire for that need to be met. This is what is meant by libidinal. He does not mean sexual desire literally, but the desire to have our need for loving-ness met.

This is a big statement to make because he is saying that the need to love and be loved will be present in every encounter, every relationship, and every interaction. He is saying that those of us who are not satisfied in our loving relationships will look for it in everything.

Again it may be that someone who has not felt loved will have developed a way of being that actually rejects overtures of affection or warmth from people, and does not consider themselves to be in search of any kind of relationship with anyone, but I think this can be thought of as a way of trying to manage the hurt and pain of feeling unloved and that beneath this tough exterior is likely to lie a deeply buried need to have some measure of care and nurture in their lives.

Even in such everyday encounters such as when the person on the checkout at the supermarket is a bit grumpy and off hand with us, we can be affected by that because we are looking to be treated in a loving way and find ourselves treated in a careless way. We may not acknowledge that we feel hurt, we may decide that she is ignorant or rude, but if we have an emotional response to her, it is likely that we are unconsciously looking to her to treat us in a particular way that would be in keeping with our own emotional needs at that moment, however much we may consciously be preoccupied with other thoughts. In other words we want more than to just have our shopping checked, we want an encounter that makes us feel like a valued and valuable person, because we do take our emotional being with us into every encounter.

If we are someone who's need to give and receive love is well satisfied, then we might not notice or mind very much if the person on the checkout is grumpy that day. We only notice and care about it, if we are looking for an emotional need to be met, along with the checking of our shopping.

A gentleman in his seventies was talking about some health problems that had developed and saying that he had attended a clinic for a scan. He was awaiting the results of the scan. He related nothing about the process of having the scan, or the possible medical implications and treatments for his condition. What he talked about was that the receptionist was very terse and unwelcoming, that in his opinion she was rude in her manner towards him. The receptionist's manner has no impact at all on the medical decisions and treatment of his condition, and yet this is what he came away with, an experience of being treated in an unloving fashion. This had a bigger emotional impact because whilst he does want his physical condition to be treated successfully, he also went there looking for an emotional experience. He was hoping to feel cared for and valued as a patient. If he could feel valued by the receptionist then he could feel confident in the treatment that the clinic offered. Arriving at the clinic and announcing himself to the receptionist was a big moment in this process and for him was loaded with emotional significance. He was in a vulnerable state of mind and was bringing with him a lifetime of hopes and fears about being well cared for, to that moment. The person of the receptionist was the person to whom all this was brought, or transferred. Had she showed interest in him, or concern, he would have felt reassured that this was a good place to be. He would have felt a positive transference to her. As it was she did not, and he was left with a wound that would take as long to heal as the medical condition for which he needed treatment. Next time he attends that clinic it will be with a different expectation, a different, negative transference. He will attend next time with an expectation that his need for a reassuring encounter will be rejected. He will attend with an expectation that the receptionist will be cold and indifferent to him. This will be the fantasy that he will take with him and transfer onto the person of the receptionist. This particular man is generally of a very robust character, not easily upset by people, but in the context of this encounter his unmet needs and hopes and wishes were revived, and these were what he brought to the clinic with him that day.

Of course on the next occasion it might not be the same person on the desk, or if it is she might be in a different frame of mind herself and be much more pleasant. This may be welcome to him but for a time it will also be a little confusing as he adjusts his expectations in line with the reality of what he encounters.

You could argue that this is not about transference, it is to do with having certain expectations based on previous experience. We learn to anticipate how things are likely to be, on the basis of how they have been, in the past.

This is true. What Freud has added to this is that we also take with us, or transfer our emotional needs on to the person from whom we are seeking something.

Sometimes the transference of these emotional needs powerfully outweighs our learned experience.

Sometimes our experience of our encounters with others is dominated by our unresolved emotional needs, wishes, and fears, and the reality is negated by the transference.

There was a story on the radio recently in which a gentleman, another elderly gentleman, had been duped into handing over large amounts of money to people who he had never met but who had told him that he had won millions on a lottery in another country. They had told him that they needed a few hundred pounds to process the payment to him. Then they told him that they needed a few hundred more for another part of the process. They continued in this way for a long time and each time he believed that they would be sending him millions of pounds a few days later and that all the delays were simply to do with bureaucracy. The police were involved, and his friends and neighbours could see what was happening, but even though he was told very straightforwardly that he was the victim of a criminal gang and had been cheated and that there was no lottery money coming to him, he continued to believe that he was about to receive this money. In the end he had paid out thousands before his bank finally refused to transfer any more funds.

This man could be thought of as having been in the grip of a transference relationship that was so strong as to have overridden his capacity to see people as they really were. It is a very extreme example and probably there is more to it than was reported on the radio, but it is an example of someone whose perception of another person was based entirely on his own wishes and desires. He wanted the criminals to be honest, and so he believed that they were, in spite of all the evidence to the contrary.

Another example would be someone who might be of a somewhat paranoid disposition. Such a person is likely to see everyone as having dubious intentions towards them. We probably all know people like this. They are always suspicious of others no matter how benign the other person may be. They are particularly suspicious of anyone from whom they may need help. They seem to think that asking for help is synonymous with an invitation to be mistreated, and that the other person will see it this way. So they distrust doctors, or lawyers, or teachers. They hate to put themselves in a position of asking for anything from anyone because they assume that the other person will see this as an opportunity to exercise negative power over them. In other words they take to the encounter with for example, a doctor, an unresolved difficulty from their own past in which they have felt that their own vulnerability has attracted abuse rather than care. They transfer onto the person of the doctor the perception that he will want to hurt rather than cure, or that he will be incompetent rather than competent. This belief can persist in the face of all evidence to the contrary. This may not seem to fit with Freud's assertion that the transference is to do with needs wishes and desires, but the paranoid person might employ this transference strategy in order to protect himself from the disappointment of feeling that he is just another patient in the GP surgery rather than a special patient.

Another person that I know was taken ill in a different country from where she lived. She emailed to relate the story of what had happened to her. At the end of the story I realised that I still did not know what treatment she had received for her illness. I knew a great deal about the nurses, doctors, and other staff in the hospital and indeed something about the other patients, but nothing at all about her medical condition. In fact she had been treated successfully and had recovered physically, so she had forgotten all about that. What she remembered, and carried with her, was the nature of the emotional contact with everyone with whom she came into contact.

The people to whom I am referring are not necessarily people with mental health problems. In fact they are people who function at a high level of competence in their everyday lives and professions. Nevertheless they bring to their contacts and relationships with others, their own emotional needs wishes and desires, in the hope that these will be met in some way by the other person to whom they are looking, for care, for reassurance, for concern.

This leads to the question of where these needs, wishes and desires come from.

There is more and more evidence that our personalities are formed in the early years of our lives, and the quality of the relationship that we have with the person who takes care of us when we are very small, is the bedrock upon which all our subsequent relationships will be based. If our first love relationship is secure and stable, and if we are well loved in a fairly consistent way that we can depend upon, then we have a good chance of being able to form stable, loving relationships with others throughout our lives. If our early experiences are of being neglected, or mistreated, or abused, we are likely to have difficulties in our later relationships. A secure stable child will know that they are loved and that their love for others is accepted and valued. This will be taken for granted. A child who is living in a neglectful or uncaring home will not know that they are loved and will not have a sense that their own lovingness is of any value to anyone. This will actually constitute a huge gap in their awareness of what a relationship is, it will be a basic fault in their understanding of how to connect with people in an enriching way. They will have difficulty in recognising lovingness when it is offered to them and will not know how to offer anything of themselves to the people with whom they live and work.

Nevertheless the need for warm enriching human relationships is a fundamental aspect of being human. It will make its presence felt, as it is the source of emotional nourishment and we all need emotional nourishment as much as we need good nutritious food if we are to be strong and healthy.

Each of us has had our own individual experience of being cared for as an infant, and it is this experience that we take with us to our future relationships and that form the basis of our transference to others. Freud based his thinking upon the work that he did with women who sought cure from their doctor. He said that the women experienced the doctor as a father figure and transferred onto him all their hopes and desires based upon the relationship that they wished to have with their father. They had a fantasy that the doctor had the wherewithal to make everything better for them, to cure them of all their sense of unhappiness. We can see examples of this in modern day life. It is not unusual for people to place their faith in someone that they believe has some kind of recipe for making everything much better for them. This is often the case with psychotherapists and counsellors, that people expect and hope that all their problems will be magically solved by the words of wisdom that are dispensed in the consulting room.

These hopes and expectations, are thought to be based on the satisfactions and disappointments of our earliest and most profound relationships with the people we first loved, usually our mother and our father, closely followed by our siblings.

Because they are based on these early experiences of dependency and the need for care, they are evoked in later life in the context of a relationship with authority figures. An authority figure is someone who is in a position of some influence or power in our lives. Because they are in this position we need them to have our best interests at heart. We have a degree of dependence upon them and this puts us in a more vulnerable position relative to them. It is this sense of them being the one to be in a position of strength and us in a position of relative weakness that evokes the desires and wishes that constitute the transference.

I have given one or two examples of how the transference works in one off encounters with other people, but how does it develop in the context of an ongoing relationship, say with a carer, or with or with a senior colleague? And can it change and alter over the course of time?

Again most of the thinking about this process of the transference on a longer term basis has been done in the context of a psychotherapy relationship, and the way in which the transference can be noticed, followed, and understood is the focus of the therapy. Equally the way in which it can alter can be observed carefully in that context. In order to outline some understanding of this I want to refer again to Freud (1914g) and his paper, "Remembering, repeating and working through".

In this paper Freud discusses the way in which people recreate old situations again and again. We all know people who make the same mistakes over and over, never seeming to learn a better way to handle things. We all know people who having made a bad choice of a partner, leave them and then find someone else, who turns out to be very like the first partner. They seem to be irresistibly drawn to the very characteristics that have caused them pain in the past. This is a kind of remembering and repeating and when a person embarks upon a therapy they bring with them this remembering and repeating in the transference relationship to the psychotherapist. Because the psychotherapist is thinking about the transference all the time they can be wondering what it is that the patient is communicating about their own unresolved difficulties from past experiences. For example if the psychotherapist is thought of as a father figure there may be an expectation that they have some kind of power to solve all problems. The patient may have a notion that they have to present themselves as a small child to the psychotherapist in order to elicit this response from the father figure/ psychotherapist. None of this would be happening at a conscious level, it would all be unconscious, but if the analyst can notice this and find a way of talking about it then the patient may be able to gradually think about their own wishes and desires in relation to their father in the past and the therapist in the present, and maybe to other people in their life who also are seen in this particular light. Then they can begin to exercise some choices about whether this is the kind of relationship that they want to be in. This is what is called working through.

But the therapy relationship is a very protected space for this kind of work and not everyone is privileged to have access to this. So we need to think about other relationships in which the transference can develop and become a vehicle for change and development.

One place to start would be that between the student and the tutor. In any new cohort of students there will be many different responses to the tutor. Some students will like her, some will not. Some students will be demanding of her time, others will be reluctant to approach her. Some will find her helpful in tutorials and seminars and others will feel that she ignores them or dismisses their attempts to contribute to the discussion. As the course progresses they will all have their own relationship with her and it will be different for all of them even though she is just the one personality. Of course this will be influenced by how she feels about them as individuals as well, but it is more loaded for the students because she is in a position of influence over their future academic success.

Of course tutors do need students, the dependency is not entirely one way, but the tutor needs students as a general group rather than as a specific person, so the transference of the tutor to the student is more diffuse than that of the student to the tutor.

What about the relationship between an employee and a manager?

John was employed by an organisation as a consultant with his own specialist expertise. He worked within this organisation for several years taking on projects. He had a very good relationship with his line manager, Rebecca, with whom he felt very comfortable. He described the relationship as being so good that Rebecca would ask his advice about all sorts of organisational matters, not just those within his particular area of expertise. This role of being a confidante to the manager was very important to John and made him feel special, though he did not think of it this way at the time.

Then the management structure changed, Rebecca was promoted and John had a different manager. Not only was the new manager (Claire) not so enamoured of John, but Claire was accountable to Rebecca and they developed a close and warm relationship, and one that excluded John. John was desperately hurt by this. He was not only hurt but felt betrayed and envious and was furious. He began to find fault with the new manager and to make complaints about her. Claire was not well equipped to deal with John's attacks upon her and dealt with John in a very heavy handed and clumsy way. Soon the whole department became embroiled in a war between those on John's side and those on Claire's side. People became ill, left their jobs and the department began to effectively collapse.

So what was going on here? There were several people who were attempting to have their own emotional needs met in different and conflicting ways. There was no one who could think about this and take this into account in making decisions about how to tackle the conflicts. There was no one who could think about what might be going on in the transference between a member of staff and a manager.

I know something about John's early life. His mother would ignore him for days at a time, something which John found absolutely terrifying as a small child. Both parents would engage in intellectual discussion at the dinner table in a way which excluded John and he would feel as though he were invisible to them. He was not allowed to have other children to play at home and visitors of any sort were unwelcome. There were no siblings.

John grew up in an apparently ordinary stable family unit of two parents and a child, but behind closed doors he was treated rather more as a thing than a person. It was a very lonely and trapped childhood with parents who did not know how to think about the emotional needs of a child.

When he took the job in this department he found in Rebecca something of the warmth and maternal concern that he had so craved all his life. In turn he felt valued by this mother figure. He hoped and believed that he had found the relationship that would repair a childhood full of longing and despair. He did not think of it in this way at all, this was all going on unconsciously. It was not until the work with him in psychotherapy began to unfold that this could be understood. But this was the transference aspect of his relationship to Rebecca that John looked to her to meet his unresolved emotional needs wishes and desires that had so dogged his life up to that point. The relationship was felt to be good and so we can say that the transference was positive.

When Rebecca was promoted and was seen to be having a close relationship with Claire, John felt once again that he had been left out in the cold. All his childhood despair came flooding back. The difference was that now as an adult he could respond with all the anger and rage that he had been too frightened to express when he had been little. He focused this rage onto Claire who then became perceived as the hated depriving maternal figure. This could be called the negative transference.

Rebecca's side of the story is not known, neither is Claire's, but it is reasonable to suppose that they too were seeking some kind of emotional rewards from their working relationships and that in doing so they too were transferring their own unresolved dilemmas onto their colleagues, particularly their senior colleagues. They too may well have been in a positive or negative transference to their senior colleagues.

The transference is not the whole relationship, it is that aspect of the relationship in which the unresolved residue of the needs wishes and desires belonging to early formative experiences is brought to, and transferred onto a figure in the present. John and Rebecca were colleagues and as such worked together in a mutually cooperative and creative way. They respected and valued one another. But John's unconscious fantasy was that Rebecca loved him as a son, this was the transference. When John had to realise that Rebecca did not love him as a son but valued him as a colleague, and also valued Claire as a colleague, John's world collapsed in a similar way to the way in which it collapsed when his mother refused to speak to him for several days at a time when he was just a little boy.

Another factor comes into play in everyday life, which is to do with the defence mechanisms that we erect against awareness of psychic pain. John defended himself against knowing about his own desperate longing for a loving mother by becoming the confidante of Rebecca. In this way it seemed to him that it was Rebecca who needed John rather than the other way around.

This is an example of a defence mechanism that can make the transference look and feel very different to that which I have described in this chapter, but it does need to be the subject of a chapter in its own right and will be addressed in a later part of the book.

The transference is usually thought of as being an unconscious process and in the example that I have used it was unconscious. But it is not necessarily so. It is possible to be aware of what it is that we look for in other people that belongs to the past. As John became more able to know about his own painful needs and wishes he became able to notice his longings and wishes that Rebecca would be able to make everything better for him. He could then begin to think that this was not a reasonable expectation to have of a colleague, and to withdraw and contain within himself, something of his "libidinal desires". He became more able to do this as a result of the work that he did in his personal psychotherapy, in which this very question of transference was foremost in the therapist's mind.

Had Rebecca had an understanding of the concept of transference then she might have been more alert to the unconscious longing that was being transferred onto her and might have been able to have a good collegial relationship without being drawn into an idealised and ultimately unrealistic one. It is not only in a one to one therapy relationship that this is possible.

In summary, I suggest there are 4 features of transference;

1. It is usually unconscious, but not necessarily so. It can be a process of which we can become aware.
2. It occurs where there is some degree of dependency or need which one person has of another.
3. This aspect of dependency evokes early, unresolved wishes and desires which accompany the sense of dependency and are

transferred onto the person from whom we need something, in the present.

4. The transference can be positive or negative. It is thought of as positive when it is experienced as rewarding and satisfying. It is thought of as negative when the feelings involved are those of hate, revenge, and rage.

This is a very simple outline of the concept of transference. In actuality it is often more complicated than this as the needs, wishes, and defence mechanisms of both sides are brought into play. It can be readily available to conscious awareness in brief contacts or in relationships in which we have little investment. When relationships are committed and long term they get complex and the question of what it is that can be called transference and what cannot be called transference becomes much more convoluted. Nevertheless the task of teasing out this question can be invaluable in making sense of the connections between people.

The next chapter will take this complexity a step further by addressing the nature of counter transference, the response to the transference.

EIGHT

Countertransference, the response to transference

The countertransference, the counter to the transference, or response to the transference, is more difficult to understand than transference, not least because there are areas of disagreement within the psychoanalytic world as to its definition.

Psychoanalysis is all about what it is to be human and since being human defies definition it is not surprising that the terminology that is used to try to describe the experience also proves difficult to define and is subject to argument and disagreement.

In this chapter I will attempt to explain broadly how the views about countertransference differ, but will on the whole be discussing my view of the concept as taught to me through my training as a psychoanalytic psychotherapist.

It is also almost impossible to understand counter transference without also considering the concept of projective identification, but Chapter Nine will be about projective processes and I am going to attempt to maintain a separation between them in the interests of clarity and simplicity.

There is a great deal of literature that purports to discuss countertransference but is actually discussing projective processes and does not offer a definition of the term. So that if one tried to identify what it is that is the countertransference component of an emotional interaction, one would be hard pressed to do so.

Once again we must start with Freud (1910d) who said:

> We have become aware of the "counter transference", which arises in (the analyst) as a result of the patient's influence on his unconscious feelings, and we are almost inclined to insist that he shall recognise this counter transference in himself and overcome it.

As with transference Freud was thinking in terms of the clinical setting of the consulting room and the one to one relationship between a psychoanalyst and a patient. He went on: "We have noticed that no psychoanalyst goes further than his own complexes and internal resistances permit, and we consequently require that he shall begin his activity with a self-analysis and continually carry it deeper."

The implication of what Freud was saying was profound. He was saying that the impact of the patient on the analyst's unconscious feelings would be so powerful that in his view it was necessary that all psychoanalysts begin their career with their own personal analysis and that they continue this self-analysis throughout their working life. He was saying that a psychoanalyst needs more analysis than most of his patients, *because* he will have to deal with the countertransference.

But he does not tell us what countertransference is, he tells us that it arises as a result of the influence of the patients feeling upon the analysts unconscious feelings.

To put this idea in another way, Freud is saying that the analyst has unconscious feelings which are aroused by the influence of the patient, and that this gives rise to the countertransference.

I want to tease this statement apart a little more and also to think about how this can apply in a relationship that is not between a patient and an analyst.

If we think back to the chapter on transference, we understood that the transference is an aspect of the emotional contact between one person and another. The person who is in the dependent position relates to the other as though they are the same as a primary figure from their early life.

Freud is saying that this experience of being treated as a transferential figure, arouses unconscious feelings in the recipient of the transference. So far so good, but he says that this gives rise to the countertransference, not that this is what we call countertransference but that it gives rise to it. We are still not yet at a definition of exactly what is the countertransference.

Indeed historically the debate about countertransference remained stuck with Freud's comments for many years until Paula Heimann (1950), put it on the map again. In her ground-breaking paper "On countertransference" she said that she was using the term to cover "all the feelings which the analyst experiences towards his patient". She is saying quite unequivocally here that the definition is simple, it is all the feelings that an analyst has towards his patient. But she then goes on to make it all more complicated again by saying that it is not just about feelings, but that the countertransference is a tool, "an instrument of research into the patient's unconscious". Now it is not just feelings, but a tool. How can a feeling also be a tool?

The history of the development of the concept has gone on in this fashion and continues to do so with no one really having been able to give a definition that can be agreed. The discussion also centres largely on the psychic activity in the consulting room between two people and has not extended very much into thinking about how these processes may take place and be considered in other settings. But I think it is possible to say that at least conceptually, there are feelings that can be called countertransference and feelings that cannot be called that. Further, I think it can be argued that it is the source of the feelings that lies at the heart of the definition. Since we are considering original sources I will use "Adam" and "Eve" to differentiate one person from another. If the feelings in Eve come from the action of Adam's unconscious upon Eve's, that can be defined as countertransference. If the feelings that Eve experiences, originate in the unconscious of Eve, they are simply her feelings and not countertransference. It may be impossible to tell where they originate, or they may originate from both sources and be indistinguishable from each other, but at least conceptually we can say that we have a definition. We can say that the countertransference is those feelings that Eve experiences as a result of the action upon her psyche of the unconscious transference of Adam.

But I would add here that as the debate has developed it has been established that we are talking about unconscious feelings and not conscious. So that we cannot say for example that we feel angry and therefore this is the countertransference, because this is a conscious feeling and in order to identify the countertransference we have to seek out the unconscious feelings. The above definition might therefore be reframed to say that the countertransference is those *unconscious* feelings that are aroused in Eve as a result of the action upon her psyche of the *unconscious* transference of Adam.

Indeed Heimann (1950) in her paper "On countertransference" goes on to say that the analyst "must use his emotional response as a key to the patient's unconscious". I would add that the emotional response of which we can be aware is the key to our own unconscious as well, it provides a clue as to what we might be seeking to know, but it is not the counter transference as such.

The next question is how do we identify what is countertransference and what is not, how do we track down the unconscious that is hidden behind the conscious, and what are the component parts of the definition?

Roger Money-Kyrle (1956) discusses the analyst's identification with the patient. Again in the context of the analytic treatment, he says that the unconscious child in the patient often treats the analyst as a parent, (transference) and that the analyst's unconscious is then bound to respond by regarding the patient as his child. He elaborates this further by saying that parents, in their parenting of their own children are as much in relationship to the early child aspect of themselves, albeit unconsciously, as they are in relationship to their actual children. This child aspect of the self is also aroused in the analyst by the transference of the patient.

Another word for this process could be empathy. Because we have all been children, and dependent and needy, we can empathise with those people around us who are feeling childlike. However this is a simplistic formulation, since whilst every adult has been a child, not all adults are compassionate towards others who are feeling childlike. Nevertheless we can add identification to the definition, we can now say that countertransference is to do with those feelings that are aroused in identification with the transference from another person.

But we are still talking about unconscious feelings so it is likely that in order to discover the sense of identification we need to explore further than empathy which is really a conscious feeling.

Let us return to the person who does not feel compassion for someone who is in a childlike state. It is not unusual for a response to vulnerability to be a version of, "pull your socks up". We frequently encounter the view that someone who is in a weakened state of mind is idle, or self-indulgent, or wallowing in self-pity. This is not an empathic response at all, it is a very critical, sometimes a very harsh response. It is also conscious, it is the response that the person is able to know about. At first glance it is not in identification with the dependent person, but is quite contrary to that. But if we look a little further we might begin to think of this initial response as being defensive, as being a protection against knowing and feeling one's own vulnerable or childlike self.

We have discussed in the chapter on defence mechanisms, the ways in which we try to protect ourselves from an awareness of painful feelings by putting something else in their place, often the opposite of what we really feel. The child who is knocked over in the playground and does not want his friends to see him crying will say and will try to believe that "it didn't hurt anyway" which is quite the opposite of what he really feels, but saves him from the humiliation of being seen to be weak and vulnerable. Equally the adult who says, "Oh, don't be such a cry baby" is protecting themselves from their own internal cries of humiliation, that are evoked by the child's crying.

This kind of defensive process may well be playing a part in countertransference so that the feelings that we can know about are simply a clue to the countertransference and we have to follow the clues back to their unconscious origin in order to discover the feelings that are both an unconscious response to, and in unconscious identification with, the transference.

Heinrich Racker (1948) discusses the needs that the analyst brings to the work with a patient. He suggests that everyone who seeks to be a therapist is hoping to be loved by their patients. This is considered to be a neurotic need that should be explored and worked through in personal therapy so that it can be understood properly. Analysis does not do away with such fundamental needs, but it does help if they can be fully understood so that they do not have to dominate the analyst's work. But when we want to be loved and are not loved we are terribly hurt by that and Racker's point is that if the analyst does not feel loved by the patient then the analyst's hatred can be aroused, and this would be a defence against feeling a sense of failure. Once again it is humiliation that is defended against here.

The point that we need to understand is that what the analyst would consciously experience would be a dislike of the patient. It would be another version of "it didn't hurt anyway". A way of saying, "Well, I don't like her so I don't care if she doesn't like me". The countertransference, which is hidden from awareness, would actually be the sense of failure, the humiliation, and the longing to be loved.

It would also be these feelings that would be aroused in identification with the patient.

A trainee counsellor wrote in a case study, about a piece of work that she had done at an early stage in her career, with a young man who was struggling with drug addiction. She had spent time with this young man (who I have called Peter) offering one to one support/counselling sessions.

Peter spent all the time in the sessions talking about his devotion to his girlfriend who clearly did not reciprocate his devotion. The trainee felt a powerful sense of frustration about the way in which the sessions were dominated by the girlfriend and wanted to try to get Peter to discuss something else. She said in supervision that she felt that she was getting to know the girlfriend rather than Peter. She wondered on reflection if her feelings of frustration could be called countertransference given Paula Heimann's definition.

I would argue that the conscious feelings of frustration and of wanting to change the subject, away from the girlfriend, were not countertransference, but were the clue to the countertransference. Some people would disagree with me and say that the conscious feelings are an aspect of the countertransference, but that they are not the whole story. In practice this is a more helpful approach to using countertransference, as it means that no feelings are dismissed from the overall picture, but it does not differentiate the specificity of the unconscious responses that need to be tracked down in my opinion. If the conscious feelings were to be explored and followed to their source we would ask some questions about where these feelings might be coming from. This is the important analytic work that is essential to discovering as full a picture as possible, to which can be attributed the concept.

Peter is deeply attached to something that seems to be bad for him. He is consciously talking about his girlfriend but of course he is also deeply attached to drugs, which are also harmful to him. The trainee wanted to get this deep attachment to something harmful, out of the way so that the real Peter could be discovered and she was frustrated by Peter's insistent focus on his love for something damaging. Peter is bringing to his contact with the trainee, an exclusive and excluding relationship with his girlfriend/drugs. The trainee does feel excluded by this but rather than admit to feeling hurt, which would feel humiliating, she tells herself that it is Peter who needs to get rid of the attachment to something damaging. This may be true, but in terms of identifying the countertransference we can see that the frustration that the trainee feels is the conscious clue to the unconscious feelings of being excluded from an intensely prized relationship. The experience of being excluded from something, and feeling hurt by that exclusion, is a universal experience and it is safe to assume that the trainee will have had her own experience of this and will have had to find ways of dealing with the pain of it in her own life. If we can think that the conscious response of frustration is a clue to an unconscious sense of identification with Peter, we can begin to think that Peter's relationship with his girlfriend and with drugs is his way of trying to find something that will protect him from the excruciating pain that he feels about living in a world where everyone else is in a loving relationship except him, and in which the person who he wants to attend to him, listen to him, love him, actually loves someone or something else and not Peter. We can then begin to understand something of the nature of Peter's early formative experiences of longing for love and of being constantly rejected.

Peter has brought his emotional difficulties directly into the room, and in doing so he requires the counsellor to experience them for herself. At first sight it does not seem that he has any dependency feelings that he is transferring to his counsellor, indeed he seems to want nothing from her, but actually he is conveying something of what it is to feel excluded and irrelevant, and this is central to the problem with which he is seeking help. But it was necessary for the counsellor to do a lot of work within herself to track down what it is that Peter is conveying because her conscious response is just the beginning of the trail to uncovering the humiliating feelings of being totally irrelevant and non-existent in the eyes of another. In going through this process the trainee has had to deal with her own experiences of being hurt by people who matter to her, and these will be stirred up in her by the encounter with Peter. In this instance the trainee counsellor had a reasonably robust sense of her own value and had been fortunate enough to have had good formative experiences of being thought about and understood and she could tolerate the way in which Peter treated her as though she was not there. Another counsellor might be different in this respect and may have found it more difficult to tolerate Peter's need to talk endlessly about his addiction to his girlfriend, rather than accept any advice about how to change his behaviour.

This brings us back to Freud's observation that the analyst can only go as far as her own defensive structures will allow her, and she must undertake a thorough going personal analysis in order to be able to understand and process the ways in which her own difficulties are engaged by the ways in which the patient presents the nature of the transference to her. He is acknowledging that everyone has their own psychological strengths and weaknesses and that because the clinician is using their own self as the primary therapeutic tool all the complexities of their own personality will be called into the service of the working relationship with the patient/client/service user.

The task for the worker in a therapeutic setting is to be thinking about their own emotional state of mind, what they may be defending against that is to do with their own internal conflicts, and from this self-examination to try to appreciate what it is that the patient is needing to convey through the transference. In undertaking this work the clinician is using the countertransference as a tool, as Paula Heimann suggested.

The trainee counsellor who worked with Peter did not at the time have any knowledge of psychodynamic thinking, but she was able to relinquish her own need to get Peter to talk about something else other than his girlfriend, and was able to resist the temptation to tell Peter that he would be better off without her since she did not seem to care for him. She was able to allow Peter to talk as much and for as long as needed to, until gradually Peter began to realise for himself that it was not his girlfriend, or the drugs that could offer an answer to all his difficulties. He began to be able to appreciate that in his counsellor he had a person who was really willing to listen to him and to think about what it was like to be Peter. This was not the perfect bliss that Peter sought, and believed was promised, in the use of drugs, but it was more reliable, more real. This gradually enabled Peter to begin to appreciate other people in his life who were not perfect, but who sincerely liked him and wanted to know him and share something of themselves with him. His addiction to the promise of a state of bliss that he mistakenly believed he could achieve with his girlfriend or through drugs, was beginning to be modified, and the possibility that he could have and make use of his own mind and think for himself, was opening up.

There is one more example that I want to describe. It took place in a care home for older people, some of whom were suffering with dementia. The gentleman that is the subject of this example was one of those sufferers.

This was an example that was also brought to my attention in an essay written by a student who I was teaching at the time.

The gentleman, I will call him Harry, was an elderly man who had seen active service in World War Two. It was not unusual for him to awake late at night when everyone was asleep in the care home, and to be in a deluded state of mind in which he thought he was on the battlefield fighting the war. It is reasonable in my opinion to suppose that he had had some highly traumatic experiences during his active service, from which he had never fully recovered.

On this particular occasion he had woken and was out of his room brandishing his stick and threatening to kill everyone. There was no doubt that he was intent upon hurting people and could have done so if the staff had not kept out of his way. The staff did not know how they might manage his behaviour and protect themselves, other than by using restraint and medication and this was what they were planning to do. They were frightened of him, with good cause.

The student, who had been studying and thinking about unconscious processes for two years, was also on duty on this occasion in his role as a nurse. He noticed the reaction of the staff and found some space in his own mind in which to put aside his fears of being attacked by Harry and think for a moment about how her own fears might be a response to, and an identification with, Harry's unconscious dread of being annihilated in the war.

This process was taking place in the space of a few moments so it was not being carefully thought through in the way that I describe, but it was happening nevertheless.

He managed to get close enough to Harry to say quietly to him: "I think you have done all you can here for now."

Harry immediately calmed. He stopped brandishing his stick and allowed himself to be taken back to bed where he stayed until morning.

I was very struck by this example when I read it as it seemed to me to illustrate rather beautifully how a capacity to think about transference and countertransference mechanisms can offer a space in which to find a way of making contact with a person that is empathic and conveys understanding. Harry was back in the war and it was his mission to fight the enemy. He did not want to hurt the staff, but he did not realise that they were staff because in his deluded state he thought they were the enemy. He did not know at that moment that the war was over and he did not have to fight any more. The student found a way of saying something to him that was very simple but conveyed that he understood that Harry felt compelled to keep fighting and needed to be given permission to stop. He was terrified that if he did not keep fighting he would be overwhelmed by the enemy, just as the staff were frightened of being beaten by Harry and his stick.

The student's intervention prevented the need for restraint and medication which would have been demeaning for everyone and would not have gone any way towards helping Harry. He did not have to suffer the after effects of medication, the staff did not have to go through the trauma of restraint, and indeed Harry could feel that for a time he had been heard and understood. The student had used his understanding of the concept of countertransference as a tool even though he had not had time to think through the meaning of his own and his colleagues responses to a dramatic situation which required a decisive and swift reaction.

The foregoing discussion argues that the countertransference can be identified as consisting of the following factors;

1. It is unconscious.
2. The conscious response of which one can be aware is the first clue in the quest to unravel the unconscious response, which lies behind the conscious response.
3. The conscious response is likely to be of a defensive nature.
4. What is being defended against, will be feelings that are in identification with the unconscious communication of the transference.
5. When this unconscious identification, the countertransference, can be tracked down and thought about, the countertransference can be used as a tool for understanding and tolerating, the nature of the transference.

If we think back to the example of John, Claire, and Rebecca in the chapter on transference, we can imagine that if Claire and Rebecca had understood something of these concepts they may have been able to ask themselves what was going on in the transference and countertransference relationships between them and with John. They might have been able to ask themselves if they had become caught up in an emotional situation that was not to do with one person's fault or another's but was to do with the impact of colleagues bringing their emotional needs to their work tasks and the responses to this in themselves and others. This might have led to a more thoughtful and tolerant understanding of John's distress, and of their own in response to him.

I mentioned at the beginning of this chapter that it is very difficult to think about countertransference without thinking about the concept of projective identification. This concept is the subject of the next chapter and is central to the understanding of the psychological mechanisms by which transference and countertransference take place.

NINE

Projective identification

Projective identification is the term given to the unconscious
processes by which transference and, in particular counter transference, come about. Like transference and countertransference
it is a concept that has developed over time and over continents,
and given slightly different emphases by different psychoanalytic
thinkers and writers. It now has a central place in the psychoanalytic understanding of unconscious communication. This chapter
is an attempt to explain the concept as Melanie Klein developed it
and its subsequent evolution to its current usage in psychoanalytic
and psychodynamic thinking today. It is based on my understanding of the term as I was taught it and have come to use it in my
own psychotherapy practice.

Melanie Klein (1946) wrote "Notes on some schizoid
mechanisms". In this paper she described the process that came to
be known as projective identification, though she did not use the
term itself in that paper. She thought, as do psychoanalysts, that
the unconscious processes by which emotions are communicated,
begin at birth and that we continue to use these fundamental
processes throughout our lives. She used the language of bodily functioning to symbolise that which she was trying to convey.

This can seem bizarre and disconcerting to someone new to psychoanalysis, but she was trying to describe emotional processes in the early infant, and a small baby's experience is entirely in the context of their bodily processes. The sensations to do with feeding, digesting and excreting are central to their gradual awareness of themselves as a being and eventually to the awareness of others as separate beings. In this early paper she was thinking about the infant's experience of having a bad internal feeling, perhaps having a pain or being hungry. She considers that the infant has a sense of something bad inside, something within themselves that is horrible, and they wish to get rid of this bad thing in way that might feel something like getting rid of excrement, a need to discharge and then experience a sense of relief and well-being. She refers to excrement as a symbol of that which is being discharged and to evoke a sense of relief at having rid oneself of what is felt to be bad. She also considers that this is done angrily and aggressively, and with the aim of taking over and controlling the person of the mother.

The mother is usually the person who soothes the infant and takes away their pain, and so she becomes the target, in the infant's phantasy, for the getting rid of the feelings of internal badness. The infant's wish is that the mother should have the badness in order for the infant to be relieved of it, and that the infant is in charge of this process, it happens because the infant wishes it to happen.

As with all things psychoanalytic, we are looking at deeply unconscious processes, and not conscious feelings, aims or desires. We are also trying to use words to describe psychological processes that take place before the infant can use words or describe in any way, their own experience. So such a hypothesis is necessarily based on close observations of infants and on an attempt to use adult language to describe pre verbal events.

Melanie Klein (1946) says:

> These excrements and bad parts of the self are meant not only to injure the object but also to control it and take possession of it. Insofar as the mother comes to contain the bad parts of the self, she is not felt to be a separate individual but is felt to be the bad self.

This quotation contains the essence of the concept of projective identification and invites careful thinking through. It is also, in my opinion, a difficult notion to comprehend, but it might help to think about how we, as adults, feel when we experience pain. We often feel helpless, and angry. We want someone to take the pain away, and we often want to blame someone for the way that we feel. We also want someone to know exactly how we feel by suffering the same painful feelings that we have to suffer. We can become quite fretful when we think that no one knows, from within themselves, exactly what this pain feels like. This not just an angry wish for another person to feel as bad as we do, but also an anxiety that unless another person actually has the same pain, they will not be able to understand our pain, and we do want, maybe above all else, to feel that someone understands what we are going through. If no one understands then we can very quickly, begin to feel totally alone and isolated.

The first reference in the Melanie Klein quote, is to "excrements". This term symbolises something that is inside oneself and needs to be discharged and got rid of. It can feel quite concrete, like a nasty lump of something objectionable.

(This is not always the case and we will consider this later in the chapter.)

The symbolic use of the term excrements is then linked to "bad parts of the self". Klein is linking excrements with bad parts of the self here but is also differentiating between them, and this is important because she is saying that we can experience our internal world in these two ways. One way is that there is a nasty object inside us that should not be there and we want to get rid of it. It might feel foreign, or it might be that we are able to recognise it as belonging to oneself, that there is an aspect of our own self that feels bad.

Klein considered that when we attempt to discharge from ourselves something that is felt to be nasty, we also feel that we have discharged an aspect of our self.

When we feel angry with someone it is often because we see them as having caused us an offence. We also want them to know, and possibly to admit, that they are the bad one, the one to blame.

A man in his seventies (Joe) told me that he hated feeling angry because it was too upsetting to him, and could recall only ever having lost his temper twice in his life. I questioned him about this as I knew him quite well and it seemed to me that some of his relationships might have been better if he had lost his temper sometimes. He said that on the two, vividly remembered occasions when he had lost his temper, he had felt that the other person had got the better of him by successfully provoking this reaction in him. He did not feel any sense of satisfaction but felt that he had let himself down by shouting at them.

Joe felt that if he became angry with another person he would not only discharge anger, but would also sacrifice his own self esteem in that process. He believed that if he discharged his angry feelings and thoughts, it would not result in just a satisfying sense of relief, but he would despise himself for doing so and would thus have sacrificed his own perception of himself as someone who did not lose control or ever become unreasonable. He may have wanted the relief of discharging something unpleasant but not at the expense of losing an aspect of himself that he valued (i.e., his self-control).

Interestingly Joe had actually suffered with chronic low level constipation throughout his life. It really was as though he had a difficulty in getting rid of something inside that felt bad and nasty.

Klein went on to say in the above quote that the intention, or the wish behind this discharge is to injure the recipient, (the object) to control him or her, and to take possession of the recipient.

We need to think about these three aspects of her thinking now.

As discussed above, when we are in pain we want it to go away, to stop. We seek help with this from another person or thing, maybe medication. If this does not work quickly enough we are inclined to get annoyed about the pain and we might blame the inefficacy of the medication or the incompetence of the doctor. We start to get angry. If we are angry with someone we want to hurt them. We are all familiar with this feeling. It may not be a lasting feeling, indeed we often feel angry and only momentarily wish to hurt the other person, because they are someone for whom we have more enduring feelings of care, affection or love. Nevertheless when we feel angry we want to hurt. Very quickly we can begin to think that it is not right that we should be suffering this pain but that someone else should be suffering it instead.

Klein says that this wish to hurt is accompanied by a wish to control. Once again she is differentiating between two feelings that go together, the wish to hurt is necessarily accompanied by the wish to control because in order to hurt someone we must effect some measure of control over their feeling state of mind. But Klein takes this one step further and refers to the wish to take possession of the other person. Imagine for a moment the experience of making another person cry. The first feeling may be of wanting to hurt the other as a way of discharging our own hurt. This requires a degree of control over the other. If we manage to hurt them enough to make them cry, we really have managed to take possession of their emotional processes for that time and inflict upon them the state of mind that we want them to be feeling. And we do this because we are feeling bad in the first place.

With these examples we can begin to see what Klein was trying to convey. First of all there is the wish or need to discharge something nasty. This cannot be experienced in isolation from a sense of discharging an aspect of the self. The purpose of this discharge is to hurt another, which involves a sense of control over the other and this involves a notion of taking possession of the other. If we make someone cry we can really believe that we have taken possession of the other person, if only for a short time.

Klein is thinking about this process as it takes place between an infant and a mother, at a very primitive level of relationship. She considered that this formed a prototype for future relationships. She goes on in this quote to say that the next stage in the process is that at that moment, the mother is felt to be the possessor of the bad object, the bad stuff that has been inside. So the process of discharge, and then take over, results in the mother/recipient being felt to be the possessor of the bad stuff that was originally being discharged. She becomes, for the time being, the bad aspects of the self. She is not a separate individual other, but she is the bad self.

I was given an example of this process recently by a friend who had spent a day in the company of a number of families and small children. There had been a lot of people milling around and perhaps it was all a bit overwhelming for one particular five-year-old little boy. It became time for him to go home and to begin to prepare to go to school the following day. At the time he was struggling with the expectations of the school that he should sit and finish his work before going off to play with his friends. He was aware that some of his friends were learning to read and write more quickly than he was. As he was getting ready to leave he became fretful and seemed to be looking for an argument. He said that he was hungry and his mother said he could have a banana. He chose the banana that he wanted, the biggest, and began to peel it, and as he did so it broke in half. At this he threw the banana at his mother and burst into tears saying that he wanted another one. He was told that he could not have another banana, but that he could have the one that he had chosen and had broken. He flew into a rage, crying, shouting, and trying to hit and kick both his mother and his father. He conveyed that it was their fault that the banana had broken, and their fault that he was now upset. He was discharging not only his own pent up frustration but also an anxiety that something might be broken inside him. Deep down he was worried that his experience of school was the result of some inadequacy in him. In other words he was attempting to discharge the sense of something broken, as represented by the banana, his rage about this, and his worry that something inside might not be as good as it should be, his anxiety about something that felt broken inside. When his parents refused to indulge his wish to get rid of the bad broken furious little boy, into them and magically provide a whole perfect boy/banana, he attributed all the badness to them and proceeded to treat them as the wicked terrible evil ones, even though it was him that was full of aggression and destruction. They had become not only the recipients of his feelings, but had actually, in his unconscious phantasy, become the nasty bad aspects of himself.

If we now go back to the term projective identification, we can consider that this little boy projected his feelings into his parents, he then identified his parents as the owners of the badness and inadequacy, and his parents became for him and for a time, the personification of that nastiness.

Thus far we have considered what Klein was conveying in the quote used above and in her thinking about these unconscious mechanisms in early psychological life. But many further questions are raised by these ideas and some questions may be:

1. Is it always something bad that is to be discharged or projected, or do we also project good feelings and aspects of self?
2. What becomes of us, psychologically, when we arrive at the end of the process of projective identification?
3. What happens to the other person, the recipient, of the projections?

We can continue to think about Joe, the seventy-year-old man, and Simon, the five-year-old boy as we address these questions and look at some of the ways in which the concept of projective identification has developed.

Klein discusses the idea that it can be good parts of the self that are projected into another person. This aspect of projective processes is given less space than the projection of bad aspects but it is important. She says that it is quite possible that just as we attribute bad nasty internal features into someone else, we might also attribute good features of ourselves to others. Or, at least, the phantasy of a good self into another. But what needs to be remembered here is that the concept is to do with the need to be in control of the other or to enter into the other and take them over as though they are not separate from the projector.

So although it may be that we project aspects of the self that might be thought of as positive, we do project those aspects that we cannot tolerate. I recently told a student that I thought she was doing very well in her studies. Her answer was to say that she was not doing as well as another student in the group who she considered to be cleverer than her. She had immediately discharged any awareness of cleverness in herself and located it in another student rather than tolerate it in herself. This is not quite the same as projection into another person, as the object of her disowned cleverness was not aware that she thought this at the time, but it is an example of denial of an aspect of the self and the projection of that aspect *onto* another. But I have also heard this student deferring to other students who are not necessarily more able than her, but who seemed to enjoy the experience of being placed in the position of the clever one as she took up the position of being less able.

She had many reasons for feeling uncomfortable with a view of herself as academically able as she was a member of a family that did not value academic achievement.

Those aspects of the self that we can tolerate we do not need to project because we can live with them reasonably comfortably, so we can own them and acknowledge the ways in which they affect our everyday lives.

For example I have a friend who can sometimes be harsh in her judgement of others and insensitive to people's feelings. If she thinks she is right about something she will attempt to drive through her point of view with no concern about causing offence. She has learned over time that she does do this and is able to own up to being like this. She can say, "I know I am too harsh at times". She doesn't like this aspect of her personality, but she can own it and does not try to blame others for any upset that is caused by her own domineering approach. In other words she does not project these features onto others because she can tolerate them in herself. She can also tolerate being told by others that she is too harsh and is willing to take this criticism and think about it.

These are examples of attributes that could be considered to be good or bad, but what they have in common is that they have to be projected when they cannot be tolerated.

Having projected aspects of the self that we cannot tolerate, what happens next? One possibility is that if we have projected something nasty into another person, we may see them as the personification of the nasty aspects that we cannot bear and become frightened of them. People who are the victims of racial abuse are subjected to this experience. They are perceived as being bad, untrustworthy, and problematic. An assumption might be made that they are the cause of some difficulty, like a shortage of employment or housing. They are then targeted as deserving of abuse. But then the abuser becomes frightened of retribution, frightened of the person of another race who might seek revenge for the abuse. The abused person then becomes someone to be feared. This emotional psychological and deeply personal process can then escalate into real violence, gang warfare, and indeed war itself.

Another consequence of projective identification can be a sense of emptiness. When we have discharged and disowned an aspect of ourselves we can feel depleted. This is how Joe thought that he would feel if he lost his temper and accused someone of mistreating him, he was afraid that he would feel somehow bereft of his own identity and that the other person would become the occupier of the rational high ground, a characteristic that he so valued.

But perhaps the most important effect of projective identification, especially at this point in the discussion, is that it can be a communication. It can be a way of letting someone know something about oneself that cannot be put into words, and having that other person understand oneself through their own emotional experience of what is projected into them.

When Simon could not tolerate a broken banana his parents understood two things, one was that they should not give into his tantrum and that he needed to be managed firmly, and two that he was feeling very stressed and that everything felt too much for him. They began to think about maybe having a word with his teacher in order to convey just how upset their son was feeling about school at this time. Simon had effectively communicated to them that his distress was not about a banana but that it was more serious than that, and that he needed their help with it. He had done this by making them feel his upset as though it was their own, but because they were able to tolerate the feelings and think about them, they did not have to also have a tantrum but could consider and discuss what their little boy was communicating to them and think about ways in which they might help him with his anxieties.

Wilfred Bion (1962) has discussed this aspect of projective identification as an attempt to communicate unbearable feelings to someone who is able to bear them and who can help the projector to tolerate and think about them also.

It is this aspect of communication that has been developed more fully over the years since Melanie Klein first wrote "Schizoid mechanisms". When she wrote that paper she was not discussing the recipient of the projection but was thinking about the unconscious processes in the projector. The concept as it has developed has come to focus much more on the impact of the projection on the recipient and their identification with what is being projected into them. Psychoanalysts have come to value the concept as a useful tool in their analytic work and consider that they can, if they are thoughtful enough, understand something of what their patients are communicating to them, by being open to the feelings aroused in themselves, in other words by understanding their own unconscious countertransference. It is the process of projective identification that leads to counter transference feelings.

It is this aspect of human communication that is considered now to be so interesting and useful. That how we feel about another person is to some extent just how we feel about them, but it may also be the result of something that they are unconsciously communicating to us. Remember the example of Peter in Chapter Eight, the drug user who so powerfully evoked feelings of frustration in the counsellor. This is an example of projective identification. Peter unconsciously projected his own feelings into the counsellor. She then became the one who had these feelings and Peter could remain unaware of his ownership of them. In this instance the student felt the frustration and thought that these were her own feelings that she had to put on one side in order to be able to listen to Peter in a non-judgemental way. In fact her feelings of frustration, were the also the result of a projective process with which the student identified.

It is more possible to notice such a process in the context of a protected space such as a counselling or psychotherapy session, but actually it goes on all the time in all sorts of social encounters.

Of course someone might be seeking to project aspects of themselves into us and we might not take that on, we might remain unaffected by it, but it is often the case that the projector will intuitively choose a person who is likely to identify with what is projected. The projection will resonate with an aspect of them and they will be more available to the projection.

We could think about a social and workplace issue of bullying for example. We often think of bullying as something that takes place in the school playground, but it also goes on in adult settings, in workplace settings, in social groups and in families. The bully assumes for himself the position of the tough frightening domineering one. But he is often a coward at heart who masks his own anxieties by playing the role of the bully. He seeks out another person to be the coward, and he needs this other person because he cannot be a bully without someone to domineer and frighten. He seeks out someone who is naturally timid and often vulnerable. Someone who already has a sense of themselves as weak will be a suitable target for the unwanted aspects of a bully's personality. The unbearable and projected aspects of the bully's internal world, the aspects of himself that cannot be tolerated because they are to do with weakness and vulnerability, are forcefully projected into another person, and the person chosen for that role is someone who does already see themselves as weak, and does feel frightened of what the bully might or does do to them. The bullied person then becomes identified with the projected aspects of the bully, which compounds their own original sense of being a timid weak person. As we know this process can be so profoundly powerful as to lead some victims of bullying to serious levels of depression, even to the point of seeking to end their lives.

Before concluding this chapter I want to mention the place of envy in the processes that we have been discussing. Envy as has been discussed, can have a powerful impact upon social relationships. It will be clear from the discussions in these latter three chapters that it has an important place in the thinking about projective identification. In psychoanalytic terms envy is distinguished from jealousy. Jealousy is thought to be the wish to have what someone else has, and it is also a fear that what they possess will be taken from them or lost. Envy is thought to be the wish to have what someone else has by taking it away from them in a destructive manner, by ruining it. Envy is the hating, destructive aggressive form of jealousy. If we feel envious of another person, because perhaps they are more clever, or more self-contained, or more at ease with themselves, we might feel disturbed, angry and very lacking in something important, when we are in their company. Some people will be able to respect this other person for their strength of personality, but others will feel diminished and will feel small in comparison. They may then attempt to discharge the feeling of humiliation that is aroused by the comparison. They may not attempt to discharge this into the person for whom they feel envy but they will try to find someone who will take on their humiliation in the hope that they themselves will then be able to feel a sense of well-being again. To give a fairly small example, the teenage youth who on walking past a smart sports car, takes out his keys and deliberately makes a deep scratch in this beautiful vehicle, is almost certainly expressing envy. He would love to be in a position to have such a car, but instead of admiring it and thinking that one day he too may be able to afford to buy one, he decides to spoil someone else's. He is not just spoiling the car he is spoiling the owner's pride in the car. When they return to their car their pride in their lovely possession and perhaps more importantly their sense of well-being, will be damaged along with the actual car.

The youth has, for a time, got rid of his envy and left the impact of it with the owner of the car, for them to feel the dismay, the anger, and the sense of injustice.

The recipient of the projection in this instance, does identify with the projection and feels the projected aspects as aspects of themselves, not as aspects of the projector.

This is the important sense in which the concept has gradually altered and come to be used in a subtly different way over the years since Melanie Klein first formulated her thinking on the processes of unconscious communication.

The recipient of the projective processes will feel the impact of them upon her own psyche and will feel the other person's projections as though they are an aspect of themselves. If the recipient is able to be reasonably emotionally mature they will be able to have some sense of empathy with the person who is needing to project difficult feelings and will be able to be thoughtful about what is being communicated. If the recipient is not emotionally mature, they will have difficulty in processing and thinking through the feelings that they have.

I hope I have been able to outline here in fairly simple terms a concept that is actually very complex and about which there are many and various understandings. My understanding is that it is the process whereby unconscious communication takes place, and that it arises from the need to communicate unbearable feelings to someone who can or will bear them. In its most destructive form, such as the bully, it is used to discharge feelings and aspects of self so that the person into whom they are discharged becomes the one in whom the unwanted aspects are located and who is then treated as the bad, nasty, object. In its more constructive form, such as the instance of Simon the five-year-old boy, it is an attempt to communicate distress to another person so that the recipient will feel the distress but be able to tolerate it and think about it and offer some understanding of what may be behind the need to discharge the feelings.

Whilst it is an unconscious process, it can be known about if the recipient is able to think through their own responses to another person and consider that their own feelings may be telling them something about the unconscious communications that are being made. It is the process by which transference and counter transference take place.

CONCLUSION

I hope that you have found this book interesting. There is much more to be discussed, read, debated, and contemplated in psycho-analysis, which is not in this book. There is much more that is not in the book than which is in the book. I have attempted to give an outline of those concepts that I think are useful and applicable to the everyday lives of people as they engage in their relation-ships with family, friends, and colleagues. I have found it help-ful and psychologically enriching to have these ideas as a frame for thinking about my own everyday life and interactions with others. If they do not help me in the immediate encounters, they help me to understand more fully my own place within a group of people and they help me to process the feelings and emotional responses that are evoked in me by other individuals and groups of people. They also help me to notice in a thoughtful way, the interactions between other people. They help me to observe and think through how people connect with each other and how they bring their own emotional selves to each encounter. It has always seemed to me that this enables me to tolerate my own and other people's idiosyncrasies, to work more effectively with the people in my environment, and to love my family and friends, more wholeheartedly than I would otherwise have done.

Conclusion

In other words my own experience of psychoanalysis has been hugely enriching on an emotional, intellectual and psychological level.

There are a number of other concepts that are not immediately so usable in everyday life as those that are in this book. Concepts such as the Oedipus complex, the theory of narcissism, the relationship between grief and depression, and how an understanding of serious mental health problems such as psychotic disorders can help us to understand more fully the unconscious psychological processes that are also aspects of more ordinary functioning. All these concepts are fascinating, thought provoking and deserving of serious consideration by anyone who is interested in how people function psychologically and emotionally.

If you are such a person, and you find that your curiosity has been piqued by this book, you may well now want to pursue this huge body of thought that is psychoanalysis and take your studies further. There are many books, papers, and courses that can offer this in many different ways and with different emphases. An internet search will reveal just how much is out there.

If this introductory book has made you want to know more then I am very pleased, for it will have achieved its aim.

Thank you for reading it.

REFERENCES

Angelou, M. (1993). The Pulse of Morning. *Poem for the inauguration of President Bill Clinton,* 20th January 1993.

Baum, F. L. (1900). *The Wonderful Wizard of Oz. Children's Classics.*

Bion, W. (1962) A theory of thinking. In: *Second Thoughts.* London: Karnac, 1967.

Bowlby, J. (1958). The nature of the child's tie to his mother. *International journal of psychoanalysis.* Vol 39, p. 350–371.

Cannon, W. (1932). *Wisdom of the Body.* United States: W. W. Norton & Company.

Freud, A. (1936). *The Ego and the Mechanisms of Defence.* International Psychoanalytic Library.

Freud, S. (1900a). *The Interpretation of Dreams. S.E., 4 & 5.* London: Hogarth.

Freud, S. (1908c). On the sexual theories of children. *S.E., 9.* London: Hogarth.

Freud, S. (1909b). Analysis of a phobia in a five year old boy. *S.E., 10.* London: Hogarth.

Freud, S. (1910d). The future prospects of psychoanalysis. *S.E., 11.* London: Hogarth.

Freud, S. (1912b). The dynamics of transference. *S.E., 12.* London: Hogarth.

Freud, S. (1914d). On The History of the Psychoanalytic Movement. *S.E., 14.* London: Hogarth.

Freud, S. (1914g). Remembering, repeating and working through. *S.E., 17.* London: Hogarth.

References

Freud, S. (1915e). The unconscious. *S.E., 14.* London: Hogarth.

Freud, S. (1916 [1916–1917]). Anxiety. In: *Introductory Lectures on Psycho-Analysis. S.E., 16.* London: Hogarth.

Freud, S. (1917 [1916–1917]). Resistance and repression. In: *Introductory Lectures on Psycho-Analysis. S.E., 16.* London: Hogarth.

Freud, S. (1917e). Mourning and melancholia *S.E., 14.* London: Hogarth.

Freud, S. (1923b). The ego and the id. *S.E., 19.* London Hogarth.

Freud, S. (1924b). Neurosis and psychosis. *S.E., 19.* London: Karnac.

Freud, S. (1926d [1925]). *Inhibitions, Symptoms and Anxiety. S.E., 20.* London: Hogarth.

Galatoriotou, C. (2005). The defences. In: *Introducing psychoanalysis, essential themes* and *topics.* S. Budd & R. Rusbridger (eds.). London: Routledge.

Heimann, P. (1950). On countertransference. *International Journal of Psychoanalysis* 31.

Kelly, K. V. (2012). Heroes at home: The transmission of trauma in firefighters families. In *Lost in Transmission.* M. Gerard Fromm (ed.). London: Karnac.

Klein, M. (1934, 1937 [1921–1945]). *Love Guilt and Reparation.* London: Virago Press, 1988.

Klein, M. (1946). Notes on some schizoid mechanisms. In: *Envy and gratitude and other works 1946–1963.* London: Virago Press, 1988.

Money-Kyrle, R. (1956). Normal countertransference and some of its deviations. In: *Melanie Klein Today.* E. Bott Spillius (ed.). London: Routledge, 1988.

Racker, H. (1948). The countertransference neurosis. In: *Transference and countertransference.* London: Karnac, 1988.

Santayana, G. (1905). Reason in common sense. In: *The Life of Reason, Vol 1,* p. 284. New York: C. Scribner's Sons.